BestMasters

Mit **„BestMasters“** zeichnet Springer die besten Masterarbeiten aus, die an renommierten Hochschulen in Deutschland, Österreich und der Schweiz entstanden sind. Die mit Höchstnote ausgezeichneten Arbeiten wurden durch Gutachter zur Veröffentlichung empfohlen und behandeln aktuelle Themen aus unterschiedlichen Fachgebieten der Naturwissenschaften, Psychologie, Technik und Wirtschaftswissenschaften. Die Reihe wendet sich an Praktiker und Wissenschaftler gleichermaßen und soll insbesondere auch Nachwuchswissenschaftlern Orientierung geben.

Springer awards **"BestMasters"** to the best master's theses which have been completed at renowned Universities in Germany, Austria, and Switzerland. The studies received highest marks and were recommended for publication by supervisors. They address current issues from various fields of research in natural sciences, psychology, technology, and economics. The series addresses practitioners as well as scientists and, in particular, offers guidance for early stage researchers.

Bohdan Popovych

Application of AI in Credit Scoring Modeling

Springer Gabler

Bohdan Popovych
Vienna, Austria

ISSN 2625-3577 ISSN 2625-3615 (electronic)
BestMasters
ISBN 978-3-658-40179-5 ISBN 978-3-658-40180-1 (eBook)
https://doi.org/10.1007/978-3-658-40180-1

This Springer Gabler imprint is published by the registered company Springer Fachmedien Wiesbaden GmbH, part of Springer Nature.
The registered company address is: Abraham-Lincoln-Str. 46, 65189 Wiesbaden, Germany

Foreword

This text is a copy of a Master's Thesis submitted to the University of Applied Sciences BFI Vienna in 2021 as a part of the Master's program "Quantitative Asset and Risk Management". This study is dedicated to my wife and soulmate Priscilla, who inspired me to conduct this research.

Vienna Bohdan Popovych

Abstract

There are several studies concerning methods of credit scoring. However, the aim of this research is to incorporate AI models to current individuals risk assessment methodologies. This is scientifically relevant within both the financial and machine learning fields, due to the increasing relevancy of AI approaches and their possible application. Therefore, the area of interest of this research regards defining which method has better accuracy of credit default predictions, based on the comparison of AI and logistic models. The scope of this study is, consequently, to investigate the capability of AI methods to accurately detect and predict credit risks based on retail borrowers' features.

The results of this research, based on the comparison of logistic regression, decision tree, and random forest, show that machine learning methods are able to predict credit defaults of individuals more accurately than the logit model. In fact, the random forest outperformed the accuracy of the logistic regression by 6%, whereas the decision tree classified data 2% more accurately than the logit model. Furthermore, it was demonstrated how random forest and decision tree models were more sensitive in detecting default borrowers.

However, in the course of the research, some limitations regarding the analyzed machine learning methods were encountered. In the application of the decision tree, it is possible to observe the lack of robustness of the model. Likewise, applying the random forest technique, it is noticeable the weakness present in its interpretability. Taking into account this limitation, the model results had to be interpreted by using local interpretation methods such as Local Interpretable Model-Agnostic Explanations (LIME) algorithm.

The areas analyzed within this research, are subjects of ongoing development. Therefore, although the thesis suggests the high performance of AI methods in the credit scoring field, further researches could lead to more in-depth and thorough results.

Contents

Abbreviations

AUC	Area under Curve
BCBS	Basel Committee on Banking Supervision
CRSP	Credit Reporting Service Provider
DNN	Deep Neural Network
EAD	Exposure at Default
ECL	Expected Credit Losses
FICO	Fair Isaac Corporation
FN	False Negative
FP	False Positive
GDPR	General Data Protection Regulation
IFRS	Internal Financial Reporting Standard
IRB	Internal Ratings-Based
KMC	K-Means-Clustering
LASSO	Least Absolute Shrinkage and Selection Operator
LDA	Linear Discriminant Analysis
LGD	Loss Given Default
LIME	Local Interpretable Model-Agnostic Explanations
MAE	Mean Absolute Error
MSE	Mean Squared Error
PCA	Principal Component Analysis
PD	Probability of Default
QRRE	Qualifying Revolving Retail Exposures
ROC	Receiver Operating Characteristic
RWA	Risk Weighted Asset
SME	Small and Medium-Sized Enterprise
SVM	Support Vector Machine

TN	True Negative
TP	True Positive
VIF	Variance Inflation Factor

List of Figures

List of Tables

1 Introduction

Effective assessment and management of credit risks are essential banking functions for the purpose of maintenance of banks' financial stability. The development of credit risk management can improve the competitiveness of European banks and financial institutions. The necessity of more accurate credit risk modeling motivates researchers to discover new methods in credit assessment. The application of artificial intelligence is one of the current trends in this area. The major employments of AI in credit risk management are predictions of the probability of defaults and the amount of loss given defaults. The focus of this research is the application of AI in PD modeling which can be employed for further credit scoring purposes.

This master thesis is considered to be scientifically relevant considering the increase of the accuracy and interpretability within machine learning models during the past years. The latest studies conducted on this subject show that Neural Networks, Random Forest, and Gradient-Boosting Machines techniques can help to develop more precise credit models.[1] Furthermore, the interpretability of machine learning techniques has increased due to the application of Shapley and LIME values.[2] On the other hand, a degree of error of traditional statistical models can cause unexpected defaults of solvent customers with high credit scores. Such credit risks can originate significant unexpected losses for banks and financial institutions. Therefore, the research aims to investigate the ability to improve traditional statistical credit risk assessment with the employment of AI techniques.

The number of financial organizations increased interest in the application of artificial intelligence in credit risk management during the last years. The first

[1] Deloitte (2020) pp. 1–2

[2] Bussmann et al. (2020) p. 12; Deloitte (2020) pp. 4–8

B. Popovych, *Application of AI in Credit Scoring Modeling*, BestMasters, https://doi.org/10.1007/978-3-658-40180-1_1

mention of neural networks as a tool for the prediction of corporate defaults was made in 1994 by Altman et al.[3] Although Altman employed logit and discriminant analysis for corporate diagnosis in his early studies, in 1994 he was one of the first who applied neural networks in corporate's distress diagnosis. The comparison of neural networks approach and linear discriminant analysis showed that in a majority of cases both methods classified highly accurately default and non-default companies. However, the research illustrates incompleteness of neural networks, when the AI algorithm assigned illogical values to financial features which caused overfitting of the model. Since that time, several researchers analyzed the accuracy and interpretability of neural networks and other AI techniques such as Support Vector Machines, Random Forests, Gradient-Boosting Machines, etc. A more profound overview of the researchers and their proposed solutions is in the following literature review part.

The research will apply traditional and AI methods for credit score model development. Credit risk assessment assumes two outcome statuses (default and non-default borrowers). This is a type of classification problem where logistic regression can be applied for. Based on the logistic model, financial and non-financial risk factors will be weighted to predict probabilities of default. AI methods selection will be conducted in the following theoretical part. Considering the complexity of interpretability of AI results, the ability of mathematical explanation and visualization of models will be a key factor for the further selection process. In the empirical analysis part, logistic and chosen AI models will be developed based on a training dataset and validated based on a test dataset. The final results of the models will be compared and interpreted based on performance metrics.

The credit risk models of research will be designed using transactional and financial data of retail borrowers. The dataset consists of individuals' default statuses, transactional information, financial and social-demographic characteristics. Default statuses were assigned to the individuals who had defaults within the last 12 months.

The research question defines which method has better accuracy of credit default predictions, based on the comparison of AI and logistic models. The research goal is to investigate the ability of AI tools to automatically detect and efficiently predict credit risks based on individuals' financial and behavioral characteristics.

[3] Altman et al. (1994) pp. 524–527

The master thesis consists of the sworn declaration, the declaration of consent, the table of contents, the list of figures, the table of directory, the list of abbreviations, the abstract, the introduction, the theoretical analysis parts, the empirical analysis part, the conclusions, and the references. The "Theoretical Concepts of Credit Scoring" includes an overview of the development, purpose, application, and regulation of credit scoring. The next part consists of the analysis of traditional statistical methods and artificial intelligence techniques, which are applied for credit risk assessment. The empirical part consists of the employed datasets overview, the empirical design of a credit risk model using statistical methods, modeling probabilities of defaults using artificial methods, models validation, and comparison of the results accuracy.

Theoretical Concepts of Credit Scoring 2

2.1 Literature Background

The foundation of statistical methodology, which later was applied in credit scoring, was developed by Ronald Fisher in 1936.[1] Fisher introduced linear discriminant analysis for the classification of groups based on the independent variables. Fisher's research defined the discriminant function that was based on a linear combination of predictors that discriminates the predicted variable.

In 1941, Durand applied discriminant analysis to classify "good" and "bad" loans.[2] It was one of the first researches in retail banking, where the author describes the effect of consumers' risk factors on the willingness of individual customers to pay off the loans. The key financial risk factors were defined as the consumer's income, amount of loan, length of the loan contract, the security of the loan, cash price, down payment, and borrower's assets and liabilities. The research described such non-financial risk factors as stability of occupation, the stability of residence, occupation and industry, personal characteristics (sex, age, and family status), and purpose of the loan. The author evaluated the importance of the suggested risk factors and designed credit rating formulae based on various combinations of independent variables. Furthermore, the research introduced the concept of consumers' classes based on the probability of "bad" loan occurrence. At present, the approaches, suggested by Durand, are widely applied in the modern credit scores models. However, the studies used personal characteristics (e.g. sex of the consumer) as one of the key factors for a credit rating formula

[1] Fisher (1936) pp. 179–188

[2] Durand (1941) pp. 44–95

B. Popovych, *Application of AI in Credit Scoring Modeling*, BestMasters,
https://doi.org/10.1007/978-3-658-40180-1_2

which will be considered legally and ethically non-acceptable in credit scoring at present.[3]

One of the pioneering studies in credit risk assessment with the Multiple Discriminant Analysis application was conducted by Altman in 1968. Altman introduced the Z-score formula for predicting the financial distress of companies.[4] Z-model describes the linear dependence of companies' creditworthiness from credit risk factors. Altman's research suggested application 22 potentially significant financial ratios as the factors for the Z model and based on multiple discriminant analysis, the author selected five the most important risk factors (Equation 2.1).

$$Z = 1.2X_1 + 1.4X_2 + 3.3X_3 + 0.6X_4 + 1X_5 \tag{2.1}$$

where:
X_1 = working capital / total assets
X_2 = retained earnings / total assets
X_3 = earnings before interest and taxes / total assets
X_4 = market value of equity / total liabilities
X_5 = sales / total assets

Altman's model defines limit values for Z-score: if Z is lower than 1.81, the company is likely to be bankrupt; if Z is higher than 2.99, the business is in the "safe" zone; the Z values between 1.81 and 2.99 can indicate that the company maintains stable activities.

Besides various studies, the development of credit risk management was significantly influenced by government regulations of credit activities. In the 1970s, several legal acts regulated the activity of credit reporting service providers (CRSPs) in the United States. For instance, the Fair Credit Reporting Act ensures that the credit information should be accurate, confidential, and relevant.[5] Based on the Act, the CRSPs have to disclose their information to the public—it increased the transparency of credit risk activities and the quality of accountability of financial organizations. The Equal Credit Opportunity Act forbids creditors to discriminate against borrowers based on sex, age, race, national origin, religion,

[3] Equal Credit Opportunity Act (1976) §1691, EU Charter of Fundamental Rights (2000) art. 21

[4] Altman (1968) pp. 589–609

[5] Fair Credit Reporting Act (1970) art. 602

and other personal characteristics which are not related to borrowers' creditworthiness when the lenders conduct credit transactions activities.[6] Therefore, employment of personal attributes as risk factors for credit scoring models and disclosure of borrowers-individuals' personal information became considered as an illegal activity.

Since the 1980s, a number of studies research the application of logit models in credit scoring. In 1983, Campbell and Dietrich employed logistic regression to predict mortgage loan defaults.[7] The authors defined that the economic variables, particularly the current and original Loan / Value ratios, were the most statistically significant factors in the mortgage classification model. In 1989, Gardner and Mills applied logit models for the prediction of defaults of delinquent borrowers-individuals based on the economic and demographic variables.[8] The studies discovered that, for the delinquent customers, the Initial Loan / Appraised Value ratio had a higher impact on potential default, than other variables, including the Monthly Payment / Monthly Income ratio. Moreover, the researchers discovered that the probability of default for the first customer's delinquency was higher than for the further delinquencies. One of the provided logistic models reached 63% classification accuracy.

Classification and regression trees are non-parametric approaches that are widely used in a number of classification models. In 1985, Frydman et al. introduced classification trees models for the prediction of corporate distress.[9] The applied recursive partitioning algorithm classified defaults more accurately in comparison to the multiple discriminant analysis. In 1994, DeVaney applied classification trees with logit regression for the identification of household defaults.[10] The purpose of the research was to analyze the predictive power of financial ratios as risk factors for retail loan defaults. The author identified Liquidity, Assets / Liabilities, and Debt Payments / Income ratios as the most significant risk factors.

Although it was mentioned that the pioneering study which applied Neural Networks in credit risk management was in 1994[11], the first application of NN in retail credit scoring occurred in 1996.[12] Desai et al. discovered that both neural networks and logistic regression models had high classification accuracy for

[6] Equal Credit Opportunity Act (1976) art. 1691

[7] Campbell / Dietrich (1983) pp. 1569–1581

[8] Gardner / Mills (1989) pp. 55–63

[9] Frydman et.al (1985) pp. 269–291

[10] DeVaney (1994) pp. 5–24

[11] Altman et al. (1994) pp. 505–529

[12] Desai et al. (1996) pp. 24–37

retail loans (around 80%). However, the NN had higher performance results in a classification of "bad" loans than the logit models. Furthermore, the authors discovered that the discriminant analysis was less accurate in the classification of borrowers' defaults compared to the other models.

In 2004, Charitou et al. compared the efficiency of the logit model and neural networks for corporate distress predictions.[13] The derived logistic regression and neural networks models had high classification rates (76% and 78% respectively). The authors analyzed also the employment of Altman's model for the prediction of UK corporates defaults and determined that Altman's model had much lower classification power than other models.

Support Vector Machines and K-Nearest Neighbor algorithms are other AI methods that can be applied for credit scoring purposes. In 1996, Henley and Hand developed a K-Nearest Neighbor model for predicting customer's insolvency and described the advantages and disadvantages of this approach.[14] At the beginning of the 2000s, the authors of several studies demonstrated that the support vector machine method was superior in credit risk classification to traditional parametric models.[15]

Based on the literature overview, the logistic regression models are used as a benchmark for a majority of the latest studies. The essential advantage of the logit approach is that parameters' significance and predicted values can be easily explained using statistical methods. Secondly, a number of the mentioned researchers showed that logistic regression models have a high classification accuracy in credit risk assessment. For instance, logit models' results outperformed discriminant analysis in many cases.

Although there are a number of studies that research the efficiency of AI methods in credit scoring, non-parametric models are still considered as "black-box" by many credit risk analysts. The comparison of AI and traditional models should focus not only on the classification accuracy but also on the ability of the models to explain how particular predictions are derived. Therefore, the thesis aims to fill the gap in the interpretability of different AI methods. The further theoretical analysis will compare AI approaches in credit scoring and identify AI methods with a proper balance of classification strength and ability to be interpreted. The next goal of the research is to test the ability of the selected AI methods to enhance the accuracy of default predictions and have a better classification accuracy than a logit model.

---

[13] Charitou et al. (2004) pp. 465–497

[14] Henley / Hand (1996) pp. 77–95

[15] Baesens et al. (2003) pp. 627–635; Wang et al. (2005) pp. 54–64

2.2 Theoretical Overview

2.2.1 Definition and Application

Credit scoring is a statistical method of classification, which is applied to assess the creditworthiness of borrowers based on their credit history, financial and social-demographic characteristics. Credit scoring is a system that is widely employed by banks and financial institutions. Designing statistical models, lenders analyze the past historical data of default and non-default borrowers and identify the importance of risk factors that influence the creditworthiness of these customers. Based on the developed models, the credit provider can predict the probabilities of defaults of potential clients using their risk-factors values. The probability of default is the likelihood that a borrower will not have the willingness or ability to pay off the loan. The derived probabilities of defaults can be applied as a base for further classification and scoring purposes. The basic classification approach assumes to define a borrower as insolvent if his / her probability of default is higher than a limit value (e.g. 50 %), whereas the borrower is classified as creditworthy when the probability of default is lower than the limit value.

The probabilities of borrowers' defaults are used as a base for credit score systems. Credit scores represent the levels of creditworthiness of the potential borrowers ranged from the lowest to the highest ones. At the beginning of the 1950s, Fair Isaac Corporation (FICO) was the first company that started applying credit score systems for loan assessments. At present, the FICO score is broadly employed by a number of American lenders[16]. In many scorecards, borrowers with high credit scores have less likelihood to be insolvent, whereas the PD increase results in a decrease in borrowers' credit scores. The FICO score system, which is used for credit cards users and auto lending clients can be represented as a range of scores (Table 2.1).

[16] Fair Isaac Corporation (2018)

Table 2.1 Relationship of FICO Score and Probability of Default[17]

FICO score	Creditworthiness	Probability of Default
800–850	Excellent	Extremely Low
740–799	Very Good	Moderately Low
670–739	Good	Moderate
580–669	Fair	Moderately High
300–579	Poor	Extremely High

Credit scoring is used for assessing the creditworthiness of individuals and small and medium-sized enterprises (SMEs) in a majority of cases. Credit scores of individuals are influenced by different risk factors compared to SMEs' credit scores. For instance, payment history, amounts owned, and length of credit history have the biggest impact on a FICO individual's credit score.[18] Modeling of SME's credit score, lenders can take into account financial and business ratios of the business, its payment history and collateral, the size, industry characteristics, and other business-related information.[19] Risk factors can also differ depending on the purpose of the loan. Therefore, mortgage, credit card, car, and student loans, and other lending services will require the development of distinct credit score models.

Banks and financial institutions employ credit scoring systems to achieve a number of business and accounting goals. First, using credit score systems, the financial companies can identify potentially insolvent customers and deny credit. Besides, credit scores support lenders in the assessment of the existing customers' creditworthiness and mitigation of the credit risks. For example, a credit scoring system can be used to develop a system of early warning signals which identify the credit risk of current clients. Second, credit score models can support credit providers in making pricing decisions. Generally, the customers with a low credit score get higher interest rates than clients with a high credit score, because "low-score borrowers" cause higher expected losses. Credit scoring models can be applied to balance credit risk portfolio and reach optimal returns on the credit risks. Moreover, banks and financial institutions employ credit scoring models to meet regulatory requirements.

---

[17] Investopedia (2020)

[18] Fair Isaac Corporation (2020)

[19] Ahelegbey (2019) pp. 7–10

2.2.2 Advantages and Limitations

There are several advantages of credit scoring in loan evaluation. The application of credit scores can allow the risk managers to automate the lending process and make it significantly faster. The credit risk assessment of SMEs based only on the expert analysis required a few working days to grant the loan. The lending process with credit score models shrank the processing time up to one hour.[20] The main prerequisite of the credit score assignment is the collection of customers' data which will be used for the model. With internet technologies application, the collection of the clients' information becomes more flexible and faster. On another hand, credit scoring increases the speed of accounting and reassessment of the existing loans. For instance, a credit risk manager can easily compare credit scores within one account and observe the creditworthiness trend of the customer. The time efficiency reached by scorecard usage influences the lender's cost optimization. As a result, a smaller number of credit risk managers can proceed with the same quantity of loan applications within the observed period. Credit scoring software can be quickly adopted by the branches' network of a lender that can increase the business efficiency of the financial company as a consequence of economies of scale. Furthermore, the application of statistical methods in the underwriting process reduces the subjectivity and bias of credit risk officers. Designing a credit scoring model, a credit manager can exclude all discriminative factors (e.g. sex, age, and race) from the set of the risk factors, consequently, they will not influence a borrower's credit score. The significance of the valuable predictors can be mathematically derived from the credit scoring model. Using the importance of the model's risk factors, the credit provider can reason the credit score's relevance to the client and the supervisor. Therefore, credit scoring can increase the objectivity of the credit risk evaluation.

The credit scoring approach has a number of limitations. First, a scorecard is complicated to use for a comparison of credit risks of different borrowers between each other. For instance, a low credit score of one borrower doesn't represent how much the credit risk of this borrower is bigger compared to the risk of the clients with higher credit scores. Second, in order to correctly predict PDs, a credit scoring model has to be highly accurate and sustainable. However, the proper balance between the model's consistency and accuracy is difficult to achieve. Bias and variance of prediction errors are indicators of the statistical model's accuracy. High bias can be a result of the application of an oversimplified model, which doesn't take into account the patterns of observations or the consequences

[20] Allen (1995) p. 23

of the incompleteness of the training data. The high bias of the errors leads to the underfitting of the model. As a result of overfitting, the model can show high accuracy within the training dataset and make poor predictions for the test data. To achieve low variance and bias of a credit scoring model, a lender can extend the size of the training data, explore various statistical and AI techniques, properly validate the model's results, make stress-tests, and develop separate models for different purposes and groups of customers.

2.2.3 Comparison of Credit Scoring and Credit Rating

Credit rating is another concept that applies credit risk analysis. There are several differences between credit scoring and credit rating approaches. Generally, credit scoring models are used for the evaluation of individuals, small and medium businesses, whereas credit rating is applied for the assessment of corporations, medium companies, sovereigns, and different types of securities. Since credit ratings are not applied to individuals, credit rating models use data from entities' financial statements, payments, business and industry-related analysis. Credit scoring can employ similar data sources for enterprises' analysis as credit rating. On another hand, individuals' credit scoring can require the analysis of credit history, financial and social-demographic data of the borrowers. Credit ratings are designed to access non-retail customers, where the credit risk per individual client is high and amount of clients is moderately low. Whereas credit scoring is a tool of retail credit business, where the credit risk per individual borrower is smaller, however, the number of customers is considerably high. The credit rating approach can include the combination of statistical models and the underwriter's judgment. Credit scoring is based, mainly, on statistical tools. Credit scores and credit ratings apply different scale systems. Credit ratings are usually represented as a numerical range or a range of alphabet labels (e.g. AAA, BB-). Credit scores can consist only of a range of numbers.

2.3 Regulatory Requirements

The Basel Committee on Banking Supervision (BCBS) was originated by the financial regulators of G-10 countries in 1974. The BCBS provides the guidelines (Basel Accords), which are aimed to increase the monetary and financial stability of banks and improve bank reporting transparency.[21] At present, Basel standards are a fundamental regulatory framework that is globally applied by banks and financial institutions. The Basel III accord consists of rules for capital adequacy and liquidity risk management. The Basel III defines:

- measures for minimum capital requirements and liquidity ratios,
- assessment procedures for credit, operational, and market risks,
- key principles and process of bank's capital adequacy management,
- the procedure of bank's stress testing,
- process of supervisory monitoring,
- disclosure requirements and market discipline standards.

Credit scoring is applied for the assessment of retail customers' creditworthiness. The Basel framework provides the definition of default, retail exposures, and the respective methods for deriving risk-weighted assets. The risk-weighted assets are part of the capital adequacy ratio, which is a base of minimum capital requirements. A credit scoring model is derived from the probabilities of defaults that are applied in functions of risk-weighted assets. Therefore, the credit scoring approach should comply with Basel requirements.

In the Basel Framework, the obligor's default is defined as follows:

- the borrower is 90 days past due on its credit obligation, or 180 days past due on the certain retail and public sector obligations, approved by national competent authorities;
- the borrower is unlikely to pay back its loan or credit obligation.

Unwillingness to pay can be determined if the obligor or the bank is filing for the borrower's bankruptcy; the bank restructures or sells distressed credit obligation; the bank changes the status of the obligation to "non-accrued" or compensates obligation's losses from bank's provisions. Basel standards specify the definition of default of retail exposures, which are the object of credit scoring. For instance, the default status can be assigned to the separate retail credit product, rather than to the borrower's level. According to this rule, a retail borrower can have, for example, a defaulted mortgage and it will not cause the default status of his / her other obligations.[22]

---

[21] Bank for International Settlements (2020)

[22] Basel Framework (2021) ch. "IRB approach: minimum requirements to use IRB approach" art. 36.69–36.72

The Basel standards specify the credit product groups that can be considered as retail exposures. The first group is loans to individuals that consists of credit card lending, auto credits and leases, student loans, overdrafts, personal credits, and other individual lending products. Residential mortgage loans are another group of retail exposures. Besides loans to individuals, retail exposures include the loans to small businesses, when the total exposure to a small enterprise is below 1 million euro. The Basel Framework defines three required subclasses of retail assets: mortgage loans secured by residential equity, qualifying revolving retail exposures (QRRE), and other retail exposures.[23] The QRRE are revolving and unsecured loans extended to individuals where the maximum total exposure amount is up to 100,000 euro per single individual. A majority of credit card lending and overdrafts with credit lines below 100,000 euro can be considered as QRRE. Other retail exposures consist of exposures that don't belong to the residential mortgages and QRRE. Examples of other retail exposures may be as follows: installment loans, personal finance, auto loans, education loans, secured business loans with exposure up to 1 million euro, and individuals' credit card lines more than 100,000 euro.

Under the internal ratings-based (IRB) approach, proposed in the Basel Framework, banks are supposed to estimate and assign loss characteristics to exposures' pools. Pools are applied to differentiate all homogenous exposures by a risk level. For each pool, a bank should estimate PD, EAD, and LGD. The IRB method requires reasonable distribution of obligors' exposures over pools. It means that every pool should consist of a sufficient number of exposures to estimate statistically representative PD, EAD, and LGD. On another hand, the bank should avoid a high concentration of exposures per pool. [24] The Basel Framework suggests the critical risk factors that should be taken into account during the assignment of retail exposures to pools: credit delinquency, obligator's risk characteristics (such as social-economical parameters), and exposure's risk features (collateral, product type, season effect, etc.). Estimation of loss characteristics requires the usage of historical data from internal, external, and pooled data sources. The observed period of historical data must be at least 5 years.

To estimate risk-weighted assets (RWAs) under the IRB approach, banks should apply risk-weight functions. There are three risk weight functions for

[23] Basel Framework (2021) ch. "IRB approach: overview and asset class definitions" art. 30.20–30.24

[24] Basel Framework (2021) ch. "IRB approach: minimum requirements to use IRB approach" art. 36.16, 36.24

retail exposures assets, according to the subclasses of retail exposures.[25] For retail residential mortgage exposures that are not in default, the following risk weight function can be applied (Equation 2.2).

$$\begin{aligned} &\text{Correlation} = R = 0.15 \\ &\text{Capital requirement} = K = \left[LGD \cdot N\left[\frac{G(PD)}{\sqrt{(1-R)}} + \sqrt{\frac{R}{1-R}} \cdot G(0.999) \right] - PD \cdot LGD \right] \\ &RWA = K \cdot 12.5 \cdot EAD \end{aligned} \tag{2.2}$$

where:
N(x) = the cumulative distribution function for a standard normal random variable
G(z) = the inverse cumulative distribution function for a standard normal random variable

For qualifying revolving retail exposures that are not in default, the following risk weight function can be applied (Equation 2.3).

$$\begin{aligned} &\text{Correlation} = R = 0.04 \\ &\text{Capital requirement} = K = \left[LGD \cdot N\left[\frac{G(PD)}{\sqrt{(1-R)}} + \sqrt{\frac{R}{1-R}} \cdot G(0.999) \right] - PD \cdot LGD \right] \\ &RWA = K \cdot 12.5 \cdot EAD \end{aligned} \tag{2.3}$$

where:
N(x) = the cumulative distribution function for a standard normal random variable
G(z) = the inverse cumulative distribution function for a standard normal random variable

For all other retail exposures that are not in default, the following risk weight function can be applied (Equation 2.4).

$$\begin{aligned} &\text{Correlation} = R = 0.03 \cdot \frac{\left(1 - e^{-35 \cdot PD}\right)}{\left(1 - e^{-35}\right)} + 0.16 \cdot \left(1 - \frac{\left(1 - e^{-35 \cdot PD}\right)}{\left(1 - e^{-35}\right)}\right) \\ &\text{Capital requirement} = K = \left[LGD \cdot N\left[\frac{G(PD)}{\sqrt{(1-R)}} + \sqrt{\frac{R}{1-R}} \cdot G(0.999) \right] - PD \cdot LGD \right] \end{aligned}$$

[25] Basel Framework (2021) ch. "IRB approach: risk weight functions" art. 31.18–31.24

$$RWA = K \cdot 12.5 \cdot EAD \tag{2.4}$$

where:
N(x) = the cumulative distribution function for a standard normal random variable
G(z) = the inverse cumulative distribution function for a standard normal random variable

If the retail exposures have defaulted, the capital requirement (K) for all retail exposures classes equals the bigger of zero and the subtraction of the bank's best estimate of expected loss from LGD. The applied risk weight functions for defaulted exposures are the same as for non-defaulted ones.

International Financial Reporting Standard (IFRS) 9 is another set of regulatory requirements which are applied in credit risk management. IFRS 9 is employed in accounting to increase transparency, comparability, and consistency of financial statements. Under IFRS 9, banks should apply forward-looking PD, LGD, and EAD to estimate expected credit losses (ECL) (Equation 2.5).

$$ECL = PD * EAD * LGD \tag{2.5}$$

In the financial statement, ECL is the present value of impairment losses caused by expected default in the future.[26] Impairment losses can be recognized on loan commitments, contract assets, financial guarantee contracts, assets measured at amortized costs, and receivables.

As a part of credit scoring models makes predictions for individuals, personal data privacy protection becomes a significant topic. European Data Protection Board is the major EU authority that regulates this issue. At present, all banks and financial companies should comply with the General Data Protection Regulation (GDPR). The document defines personal data such as all genetic, mental, cultural, economic, and social identity individuals' information.[27] The object of the GDPR is the sensitive data of EU citizens. Thus, all EU and non-EU companies that use the personal data of EU individuals must obtain the individuals' consent to process their data. Moreover, the users may request a bank or a financial company to provide a copy of their data or eliminate the users' information from the financial entity's records.

[26] IFRS 9

[27] GDPR art. 4

Credit Scoring Methodologies 3

3.1 Traditional Credit Scoring Techniques

Generally, traditional methods in credit scoring consist of linear methods and expert-based opinion approaches. Linear methods are a parametric approach, where a linear combination of independent features is used for the representation of a dependent variable. In credit scoring, independent parameters are risk factors, and a dependent variable is PD or creditworthiness level. Discriminant analysis is the first linear approach that was applied for credit scoring purposes. Logistic regression is a type of generalized linear model, which is widely applied for classification tasks. Based on the research overview, the logistic regression method is considered to be the standard of traditional credit scoring. On another hand, banks and financial companies develop expert systems for credit risk assessment. Expert systems do not use statistical models and are, mainly, based on a set of underwriting rules and procedures.

3.1.1 Discriminant Analysis

In credit scoring, linear discriminant analysis (LDA) is applied to identify the discriminate parameters that differentiate two or more groups of creditworthiness (e.g. default and non-default). The LDA aims to maximize the separation between distressed and creditworthy entities using the linear combination of the most significant factors. The discriminant analysis can distinguish between different levels of creditworthiness, however, the basic approach requires at least two classes, such as default and non-default customers. In order to derive the maximum split, LDA requires to maximize the distance between the classes' means and minimize

B. Popovych, *Application of AI in Credit Scoring Modeling*, BestMasters,
https://doi.org/10.1007/978-3-658-40180-1_3

the variation within each group simultaneously.[1] For the two group discrimination task, the following maximization function can be applied (Equation 3.1).

$$\underset{\hat{w}}{max}\ \gamma = \frac{(\bar{\mu}_1 - \bar{\mu}_0)^2}{\overline{s_1^2} + \overline{s_0^2}} \leftarrow \frac{maximize\ between\ groups\ distance}{minimize\ within\ groups\ distance} \tag{3.1}$$

where:

$\bar{\mu}_1,\ \bar{\mu}_0$ = means of groups

$\overline{s_1^2},\ \overline{s_0^2}$ = variations ("scatters") of groups

γ = discriminant indicator (eigenvalue)

$\hat{w}$ = estimates of the parameters' weights

Figure 3.1 illustrates an example of a distribution of two classes (e.g. default and non-default) based on two parameters (X_1 and X_2). The goal of LDA is to find the vector which maximizes the separation between default and non-default values and minimizes the scatters of each of the groups.

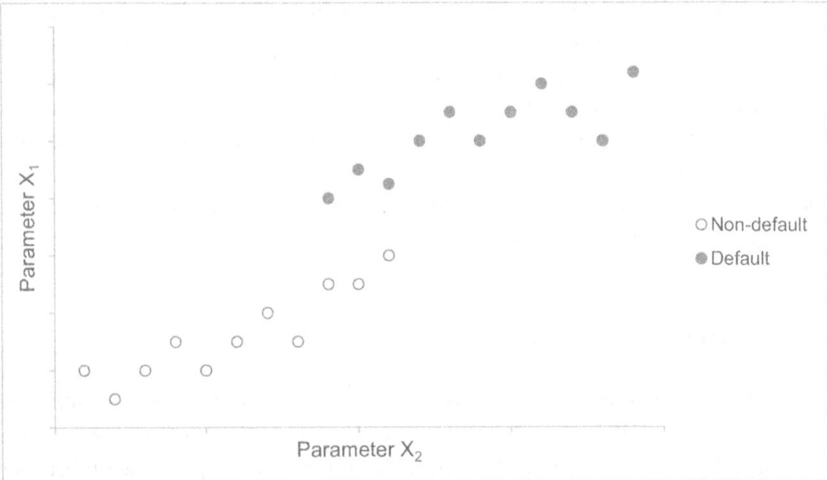

Figure 3.1 Distribution of Default and Non-default Values Based on two Parameters

In order to create the discriminant vector, LDA projects all data from parameters X_1 and X_2 onto the new axis. Figure 3.2 demonstrates the process of

[1] Balas et al. (2020) pp. 31–54

projection of the data onto the discriminant vector. Although the data can be projected onto a number of axes, the goal of LDA is to find such a vector where the function maxS (3.1) will reach its maximum. Figure 3.3 illustrates the discriminant vector with minimized within-class scatters s_0^2 and s_1^2 for the analyzed example and the respective maximum between-groups distance of the projected values.

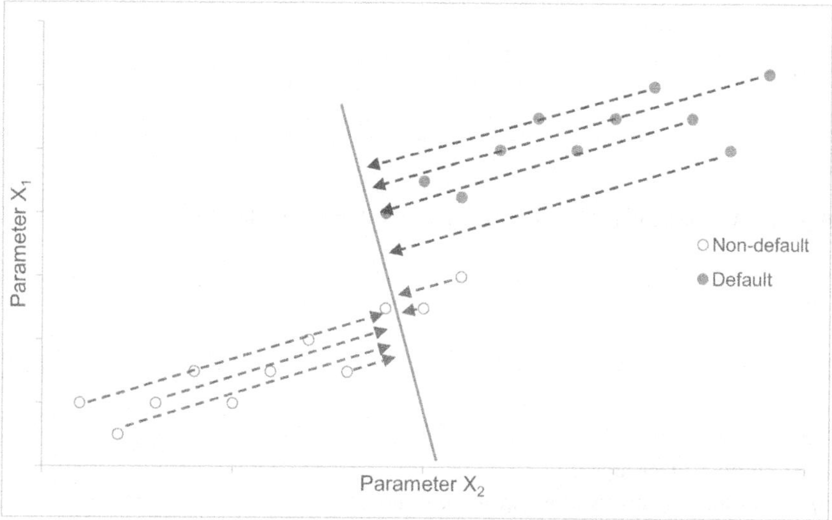

Figure 3.2 Projection of Default and Non-default Values onto the new axis

For the LDA with more than two classes (e.g. credit scores groups), the distance between means will be estimated differently. First, the analyst has to define the mean of all means and after calculate the distance of each mean to the "central" mean. The concept of the maximization function stays similar: maximize the distance between each class and the "central" mean, while minimizing the within groups variations. The between-group distance for multiple groups can be represented as the following function (Equation 3.2).

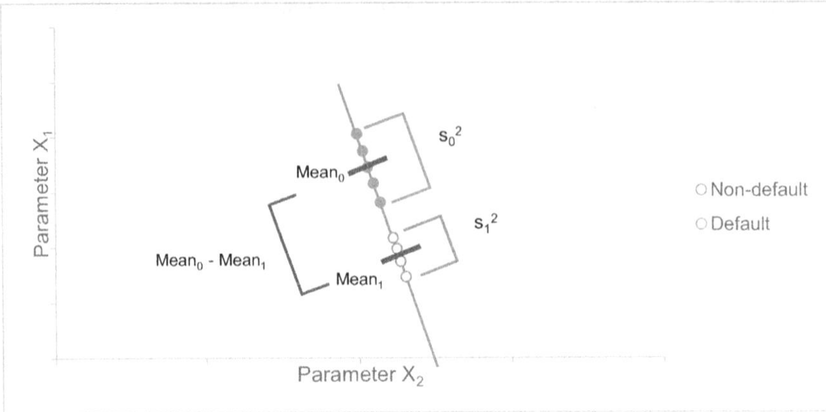

Figure 3.3 Illustration of between-groups and within-groups distances

$$S_{between} = \sum_{k=1}^{m} n_k(\mu_k - \mu)(\mu_k - \mu)^T \tag{3.2}$$

where:
m = number of groups
n_k = number of observations in the k-th group
μ_k = mean of the k-th group
μ = mean of all means (the "central" mean)

For the calculation of within groups scatters for multiple groups, where x_{ik} is the i-th value from the k-th group, the following function can be applied (Equation 3.3).

$$S_{within} = \sum_{k=1}^{m} \sum_{i=1}^{nk} (x_{ik} - \mu_k)(x_{ik} - \mu_k)^T \tag{3.3}$$

For the multiclass discriminant problem, the following maximization problem can be applied (Equation 3.4).

$$\max_{\hat{w}} \gamma = \frac{S_{between}}{S_{within}} \leftarrow \frac{maximize\ between\ groups\ distance}{minimize\ within\ groups\ distance} \tag{3.4}$$

To estimate the parameters' weights ($\hat{w}$) that are applied for the discriminant function, the maximization function can be represented as the following equation (Equation 3.5).

$$\hat{w} = \max_{\mathrm{w}} \frac{\mathrm{w}^T \mathrm{S}_{between} \mathrm{w}}{\mathrm{w}^T \mathrm{S}_{within} \mathrm{w}} \tag{3.5}$$

Based on the estimated coefficients, the discriminant score of a discriminant function for default and non-default entities can be derived using the following formula (Equation 3.6).

$$Z = \hat{w}^T X + C \tag{3.6}$$

where:
X = independent variables values
$\hat{w}$ = estimated weights of independent variables
C = biased constant

To derive reliable results, several assumptions of LDA should be met. Within the first assumption, within-group variances should be homogenous. Therefore, to avoid heteroscedasticity, variances have to be the same for all levels of independent variables. The second assumption is about multivariate normal distribution within classes. It supposes that predictors have to be normally distributed within all groups. Within the third assumption, multicollinearity has to be absent. The high correlation between independent variables decreases the classification's accuracy. The last assumption is about the independence of observations: each observation of the sample should not be influenced or defined by the other observations.[2]

There are several advantages of LDA application in Credit Scoring. The first benefit of discriminant analysis is simplicity in estimation and representation of results. The discriminant function requires only linear computations and can be defined as a linear formula with weights of predictors. The second advantage is that LDA can have high predictive power when its assumptions are met. Based on the several studies mentioned in the literature overview section, LDA had high performance. For instance, the Altman Z-score model was a benchmark for a long time in the finance industry. Moreover, the LDA can show high efficiency not only with big training datasets but also with little samples. The major limitations of LDA in Credit Scoring are defined by its strict assumptions. For example,

[2] Liong / Foo (2013) p. 1160

the assumption about multivariate normality is rarely met in the real financial world. As a consequence, LDA has also high sensitivity to outliers that decreases its predictive power. To summarize, LDA application in credit scoring is not expedient, when any predictors are not normally distributed.

3.1.2 Logistic Regression

Logistic regression is a linear classifier that is used for the analysis of relationships between predictors and a dependent variable. The logit's outcome is defined by the sum of products of coefficients and the respective inputs; consequently, the logit model belongs to the group of generalized linear models. Logit regression is used for the classification of categorical variables. In credit scoring, the binary logit model is widely applied for classification default and non-default values. The general form of the regression model can be represented as the following equation (Equation 3.7).

$$y = F(x_1, x_2, \ldots, x_n) \tag{3.7}$$

The linear combination of parameters of logit regression can be represented as the following function (Equation 3.8).

$$y = \beta_0 + \beta_1 X_1 + \ldots + \beta_n X_n \tag{3.8}$$

where:
y = dependent variable
X_i = independent variables' values
β_i = weights of independent variables
β_0 = biased constant
n = number of independent variables

The general equation of the logit model (3.8) looks in the same way as the functions of linear regression and LDA. However, the major difference of logistic regression from linear regression is that the output y of the function (3.8) is defined as log-odds of the default event. The log-odds function can be illustrated in the following expression (where p is PD) (Equation 3.9).

$$\ln(\frac{p}{1-p}) = \beta_0 + \beta_1 X_1 + \ldots + \beta_n X_n \tag{3.9}$$

where:
$0 < p < 1$

The logit model will reach its maximum precision when the best fitting line of log-odds will be found. If the probability of default (p) equals 1 and the probability of non-default equals 0, log-odds of default and non-default observations can be estimated using the following calculations (Equation 3.10 and Equation 3.11).

$$p = 1 \rightarrow \ln(\frac{1}{1-1}) = \ln(\frac{1}{0}) = \ln(1) - \ln(0) \leftrightarrow streams\ to\ positive\ infinity \tag{3.10}$$

$$p = 0 \rightarrow \ln(\frac{0}{1-0}) = \ln(\frac{0}{1}) = \ln(0) \leftrightarrow streams\ to\ negative\ infinity \tag{3.11}$$

The following graph shows an example of the fitting line for the univariate logistic model with the parameter X_1 (Figure 3.4).

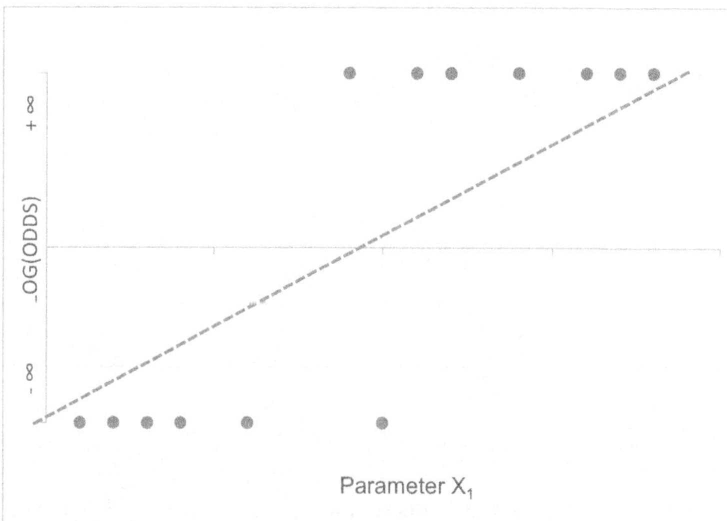

Figure 3.4 Log-odds fitting line for the univariate logit regression

The log-odds of the inputs can be defined by the projection of the input on the fitting line. Using log-odds values, it is possible to derive the estimated probability of default. Based on the vectors of input values and their weights, the probability of default can be defined using the next formula (Equation 3.12).

$$p = \frac{e^{\log(odds)}}{1 + e^{\log(odds)}} = \frac{e^{\log(\hat{w}^T X + C\ )}}{1 + e^{\log(\hat{w}^T X + C\ )}} \tag{3.12}$$

where:
X = independent variables values
$\hat{w}$ = estimated weights of independent variables
C = biased constant

An example of the classification curve with the estimated probabilities of defaults for the analyzed univariate regression is illustrated in Figure 3.5.

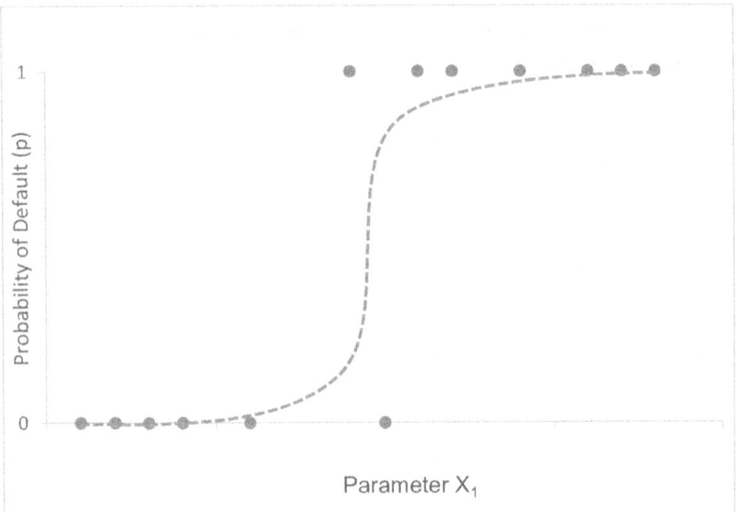

Figure 3.5 Logit classification curve for the univariate regression

To find the best fit of the log-odds function (Figure 3.4), the sum of log-likelihoods of each individual *odds*-value (Equation 3.12) should be maximized. The squiggle with the maximum likelihood will reach its maximum classification power.

There are several assumptions of logistic regression that should be followed. First, the dependent variable should be represented in a binary way (e.g. 1 for default, 0 for non-default) or as categories (for ordered logit regression). Therefore, the binary logit model follows the Bernoulli distribution. Second, there should be linear relationships between the predictors and log-odds. Third, all events of the model's sample should be independent of each other. Thus, an observation should not be influenced by other observations. Fourth, multicollinearity between independent variables should be reduced. Finally, the logistic regression usually requires a large dataset for proper model fitting. For instance, the number of events should be more than the number of predictors.

There are several advantages and limitations of logit regression. Logistic regression is efficient in training and clear in the interpretation of the results. The majority of studies in the literature overview demonstrated that logistic regression had high classification accuracy in predicting default events. Second, compared to LDA and linear regression, logit regression has much fewer assumptions: no normal distribution of errors is required; no requirements of homoscedasticity; relationships between predictors and estimated probabilities should not be linear.[3] Another advantage of the logistic regression is that its output probability is always in the range between 0 and 1, despite a range of the input values. The weights and linear representation of features allow analysts to interpret the importance of logit's predictors. One of the limitations of logistic regression is that it doesn't describe complex non-linear relationships between independent and dependent variables. There could be some important risk factors, but if there are no linear relationships between these factors and log-odds of default, these features will not be considered. As result, the model can be "underfitted". Another limitation of logit regression is that it requires a large size of training data to provide reliable results. Besides, logistic regression is quite sensitive to outliers and extreme values.

3.1.3 Expert Systems

The expert system is an automated decision-support tool based on the knowledge and experience of experts. An expert system can be applied in credit scoring for supporting credit decisions. It can be designed as the set of rules and logical requirements to classify the level of creditworthiness of a borrower. The major difference of expert systems from generalized linear models is that the rules and conditions are not based on statistical analysis, but the expert's opinion. In credit scoring, the role of the expert can belong to the credit risk analyst/manager who

---

[3] Schreiber-Gregory (2018) p. 4

has appropriate skills and knowledge in the underwriting process. The expertise of the underwriter can be grouped as a knowledge base of the expert system. Thus, the knowledge base should include the best credit assessment practice.[4] The relationships between the knowledge base and data inputs (e.g. economic and social borrower's characteristics) can be described through the inference engine. The inference engine is a set of rules and conditions that are used for the classification of the outputs. The inference engine usually consists of the set of the "if…then…" statements. The following sentence can be an example of the conditional statements: "if the annual gross income of the borrower < 10,000 euro, then the borrower has low creditworthiness". Generally, the inference engine is processed by computers, which allows analysts to quickly classify the borrowers. Another component of expert systems is an explanation mechanism that describes how the recommended outputs were derived based on a knowledge base and input values.[5] Thus, the process and results should be documented for reproduction and accounting purposes. The form of expert system outputs differs from the standard form of statistical outputs. Instead of PD estimation and further PD conversion to credit scores, the expert systems assign credit scores immediately.

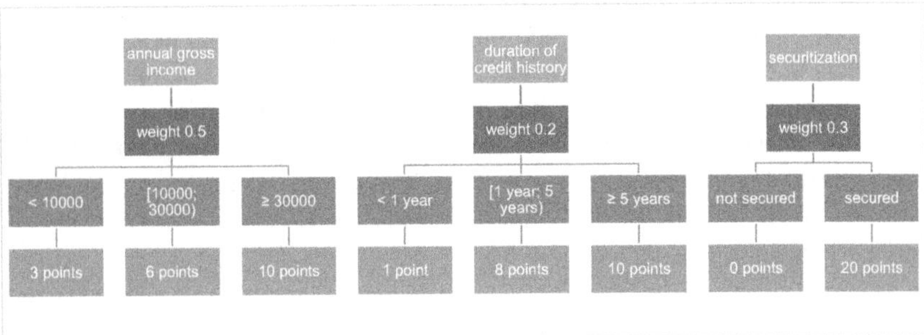

Figure 3.6 Example of a basic inference engine

Figure 3.6 illustrates an example of a credit scoring interference engine with three parameters (annual gross income, duration of credit history, securitization). The green layer represents "if" logical statements. For example, the annual gross income of a borrower can be assigned to the three groups depending on its size: less than 10,000 euro; income between 10,000 euro and 30,000 euro; more or

[4] Tripathi (2011) p. 19

[5] Alma et al. (2014) pp. 62–63

equal than 30,000 euro. The groups can be also based on categorical values, such as secured and not secured loans. Depending on the assigned if-group, the borrower receives the points of creditworthiness. For instance, higher annual gross income leads to a bigger amount of points; not secured loans receive 0 points while secured ones receive 20 points. The final step is to multiply the output values by the respective weights. In this example, gross income parameters have the largest weight (0.5), while the weight of duration of credit history is the smallest one (0.2). The maximum possible credit score can be calculated using the following equation and maximum input values (Equation 3.13).

$$\text{Credit score} = w_1 x_1 + \ldots + w_n x_n \quad == 0.5{*}10 + 0.2{*}10 + 0.3{*}20 = 13 \tag{3.13}$$

where:
w_i = weights of the parameter i
x_i = input of parameters i
n = number of i_{th} parameters

Based on the provided expert system, if the borrower has 20,000 gross annual income, 2 years of credit history, and his / her loan is secured, then his / her credit score is estimated to be 10.6 (Equation 3.14).

$$\text{Credit score} = w_1 x_1 + \ldots + w_n x_n \quad == 0.5{*}6 + 0.2{*}8 + 0.3{*}20 = 10.6 \tag{3.14}$$

The expert systems differ significantly from statistical methods. In expert systems, the logic of the relationships is not explained by correlations and statistical ratios, but by the people's expertise in the domain. This difference defines the advantages and disadvantages of this approach. One of the advantages is the simplicity in computation and representation of results. For example, the classification can be represented as a logical tree with clear relationships between inputs and outputs. The second benefit of expert systems is flexibility. The expert approach makes it possible to customize the model to the particular credit product with an unlimited amount of conditions. This technique allows analysts to describe both linear and non-linear relationships. The third advantage is that the expert system can be efficient with the lack or even absence of the training data.

High dependence on the knowledge base, causes a number of limitations of expert systems. First, the knowledge base acquisition, maintenance, and sharing require big efforts. The experts should always increase their knowledge in the domain, update the knowledge base, and effectively share their knowledge with others. It requires frequent manual updates of the rules and conditions because the domain's knowledge base and market conditions are changing constantly. Furthermore, the expert systems are difficult to scale, as it requires a lot of experts' resources. Finally, the expert systems increase the subjectivity of the analysis. The biased approach can cause discrimination risks.

3.2 Artificial Intelligence Classification Methods

Artificial intelligence is a field of various methods for solving tasks that require human cognitive skills. At present, AI is widely applied in several life areas. For example, AI detects spam emails, recognizes objects in pictures, makes sales forecasts, customizes advertising programs, analyses documents' content, drives cars, predicts the risks, etc. In the financial industry, AI is applied in credit, market, operational risk detection, asset prices predictions, customers demand forecasting, costs optimization, financial planning, document processing, chatbots, customer signification, ATMs cash-flow optimization, and many other fields. The latest increase of demand in AI can be explained by:

1) The growth of data availability, as a consequence of the digital revolution.
2) The development of computer capabilities, which increases the speed of computational processes.
3) The discovery and application of innovative artificial intelligence algorithms.

Depending on application areas, there are such types of AI as pattern recognition, speech recognition, natural language processing, and object recognition as a part of computer vision. As a subfield of AI, machine learning is a technique that automatically discovers data patterns without required programming. Machine learning can be categorized by supervised, unsupervised, and reinforcement learning. Supervised learning requires the past historical values of a dependent variable for the model training. Unsupervised learning splits the data into groups based on the data patterns without a predefined dependent variable. Reinforcement learning consists of algorithms that learn by the experience of the previous wins and failures to reach a specific goal. Deep learning is a subarea of machine learning that aims to perform tasks, mimicking human cognitive processes.[6] Artificial neural networks, which are examples of deep learning, designed as an imitation of a

[6] Du et al. (2016) pp. 159–164

net of the human brain's neurons. These artificial neurons receive data inputs, process them, and send the output to the further activated neurons.

Based on the goal of analysis, AI can be used for classification and prediction tasks. The main difference between these two approaches is that the prediction's dependent variable consists of continuous data and the classification dependent variable employs categorical data. The task of classification is to separate the observations into groups. On another hand, the goal of prediction is to fit predicted values to the real data. Examples of prediction tasks can be option price forecasting or the company's revenue prediction. Credit scoring is an example of a classification process because defaults and non-defaults are categorical values that should be recognized. Therefore, in further analysis, AI classification methods will be compared.

3.2.1 Overview of AI Classification Techniques

In this chapter, the major supervised, unsupervised, and reinforcement machine learning models will be analyzed. Based on the features of the proposed methods, the most relevant AI techniques will be selected for further extended theoretical and empirical analysis.

Decision Trees, Random Forest, Gradient Boosting, Deep Neural Networks, and Support Vector Machines are the most used supervised methods for classification tasks. Such algorithms as Random Forest and Gradient Boosting belong to the group of classification-trees-based methods. Deep Neural Networks belong to the group of deep learning algorithms because they are based on complex structures of neurons with hidden layers. Support Vector Machines (SVMs) belong to Statistical Learning Theory that is intended to formalize the process of inductive inference using statistical analysis.[7] K-Means-Clustering (KMC) is an example of unsupervised learning, which is trained on unlabeled observations (e.g. without default and non-default statuses).

Deep Neural Networks

Deep Neural Network (DNN) is an AI approach that analyzes data flow in a structured way imitating the human brain processes. DNNs are considered non-linear machine learning tools. DNN consists of input, hidden, and output layers of neurons. The training data is transferred through the input neurons to the neurons of hidden layers. In the next step, neurons of hidden layers are trying

[7] Bousquet et al. (2003) p. 176

to recognize some patterns and connections between features and the dependent variable. Mathematically, every "hidden neuron" is represented with an activation function (e.g. logistic function) and weights of input data.[8] As a result, these neurons receive input data, process it, and transfer outputs to the next layers. The output layer is the last layer of DNN. In credit scoring, the output layer can be represented as PD estimates. The estimates of the output layer are compared with the actual data and the model's error is calculated. Using the back-propagation method DNN adjusts the weights of the neurons in the hidden layers to decrease the contributions of these neurons to the model's error. The process of DNN learning is based on many forward and backward propagation iterations.

Empirical studies in different fields show the high performance of DNN. One of the explanations of its success can be the ability of DNN to detect complex non-linear patterns of data with a large number of parameters and observations. On another hand, the complex structures with multiple layers of neurons decrease the interpretability of model results. Another limitation of DNN is that its learning process is quite time-consuming and requires a lot of computing power.

Classification-Tree-Based Methods

Classification (Decision) Tree is a schematic machine learning method that can be illustrated in a tree-shape way and applied for the classification of events. In credit scoring, classification trees can be used for PD estimation. The decision tree algorithm finds the strongest separators among model parameters and, adding each next separator, improves the "purity" of the divided groups. Decision trees are highly interpretable as analysts can easily illustrate the classification process and logically explain the impact of parameters. At the same time, a number of empirical studies demonstrate that the application of decision trees frequently leads to overfitted models.

Random Forest is a tree-based machine learning model that is based on the concept of aggregation of results of multiple randomly designed trees. The generation of hundreds of uncorrelated trees allows the random forest to decrease the model's variance.[9] To construct a number of diverse trees, random forest randomly selects a part of observations and a part of features from the training dataset as a subsample for each decision tree. In order to classify new events, every decision tree makes a prediction and a random forest provides the aggregated result of all trees (e.g. mean). The random forest has high performance, however, this method is considered as a "black-box" approach.

---

[8] Fathi / Shoja (2018) pp. 299–305

[9] Friedman et al. (2001) p. 312

Gradient Boosting is another ensemble approach based on decision trees. Unlike the random forest algorithm, gradient boosting does not create multiple random trees simultaneously, but adds decision trees stepwise, reducing model loss.[10] Each added decision tree focuses on the prediction of the observations where the previous decision trees performed poorly. With every step, Gradient Boosting decreases variance and bias contemporary. The process is repeated until the addition of a new decision tree improves the accuracy of the model. Finally, all individual decision trees are combined in an ensemble which is used for further classification. Gradient Boosting is considered a powerful classification method. On another hand, its interpretability of model results is low. Low interpretability is also caused by a big number of hyperparameters (e.g. learning rate, number of trees) that have to be tuned manually and can have a big impact on the model's structure.

Support Vector Machines

The objective of Support Vector Machines (SVMs) is to identify a separating hyperplane that maximizes the distance between two classes. Support vectors represent vectors with the closest data observations to a hyperplane. SVM aims to find the optimal directions and positions of the support vectors based on the distance between these vectors and the model's classification accuracy. The SVM's classifier is a hyperplane that is located in the middle between support vectors. If there are no linear relationships between independent variables and a dependent variable, SVM projects observations onto higher-dimensional space, where it is possible to separate the data linearly with a hyperplane. Then, an increase in dimensionality allows SVM to classify the data based on its non-linear patterns.[11] Generally, SVM is a powerful tool for classification problems that shows a good performance. On another hand, it is difficult to interpret the weights and impact of variables of non-linear SVM models.

K-Means-Clustering

Clustering algorithms are used when the classes are not predefined. Therefore, the object of clustering is to find some similarities between the observations and join similar observations into groups. By maximizing the observations similarity within clusters, the algorithm aims to make the clusters more diverse among themselves. The goal of K-means-clustering is to split all data into k-number of clusters to classify the data. To cluster the data, the K-means method randomly

---

[10] Ye et al. (2009) pp. 2061–2064

[11] Suykens (2001) pp. 287–294

selects k-number observations and measures the distance of all other observations to the selected k-data-points. Next, all observations are assigned to the k-clusters based on the nearest distances to the random k-points. Finally, means of k-clusters are estimated and all observations are reassigned to k-clusters based on the nearest distances to the k-clusters means. The process of the selection of random observations and k-clustering is repeated multiple times to find clusters with the lowest total variation within groups. The major advantage of unsupervised methods and k-means-clustering particularly is that these models can describe the existing data even without borrowers' creditworthiness information. For example, borrowers with similar patterns can be quickly identified and analyzed. On another hand, clusters do not provide any information about the PD of borrowers. Another limitation of the k-means-clustering model highly depends on the size of the k-value and the k-number should be chosen manually.

Performance and Interpretability of AI

According to the goal of this research, the investigation of the accuracy of AI techniques in credit scoring is the research's priority. Higher precision of credit risk prediction can allow a creditor to decrease its losses. At the same time, to ensure the robustness of credit scoring models, the models' results must have a clear interpretation.

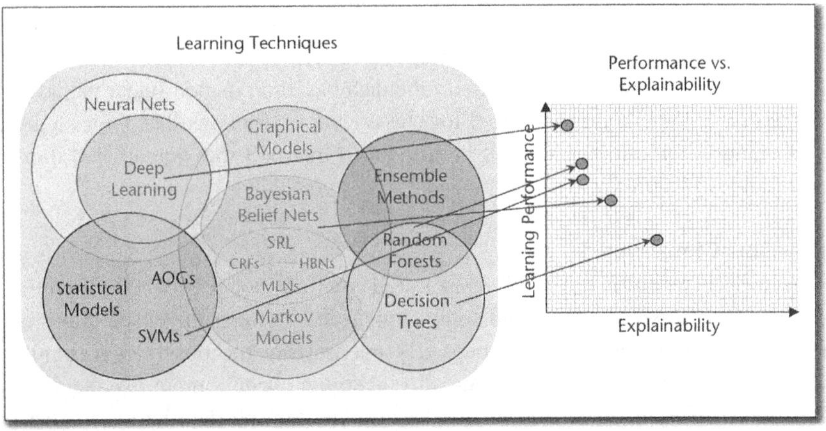

Figure 3.7 AI Models Comparison Based on Explainability and Performance Accuracy[12]

[12] Gunning / Aha (2019) p. 46

Based on the previous overview, several machine learning approaches with high performance tend to have low interpretability (e.g. deep neural networks, SVMs, random forests). Some other methods, such as decision trees, are easy to explain but may have lower performance due to overfitting. Figure 3.7 illustrates the trade-off between interpretability and accuracy of AI techniques. Nevertheless, numerous empirical studies show that the accuracy of the suggested AI methods highly depends on data and fields of research. and there is no universal technique that presents the highest performance.

The following parts of the research will focus on decision trees and random forest algorithms. The decision trees method was chosen for further analysis because it has higher explainability compared to many other AI methods. The choice of random forest technique was predetermined by its high performance in classification tasks. Both these methods will be profoundly researched and compared to the logistic regression method based on the empirical analysis.

3.2.2 Decision Trees

The decision tree is a machine learning approach that is widely applied for classification tasks. A decision tree can be illustrated as a hierarchical structure with classification rules. The logical rules of decision trees are similar to the rules of expert systems: observations are classified based on "if... then..." statements. However, in decision trees, the choice of classifiers and their limit values is conducted automatically based on their statistical importance. The decision tree starts with the most important classifier (the root node of the tree) splitting all dependent values into two groups (true or false). All following lower classifiers (if-statements) are called "internal nodes". Lastly, all dependent values are assigned to the respective then-statements groups, which are called "leaves".

Figure 3.8 shows an example of a decision tree for credit-default classification. In this example, annual gross income is selected as a root node. The securitization parameter can be an example of an internal node. The final "green nodes" with numbers of default and non-default values are leaves. The logics of this decision tree can be formulated in the following way:

- if the annual gross income of the borrower is equal to or higher than 10500 euro, then the PD is 6%;
- if the annual gross income of the borrower is lower than 10500 euro and the loan is secured, then the PD is 2%;

- if the annual gross income of the borrower is lower than 10500 euro and the loan is not secured, then the PD is 89%.

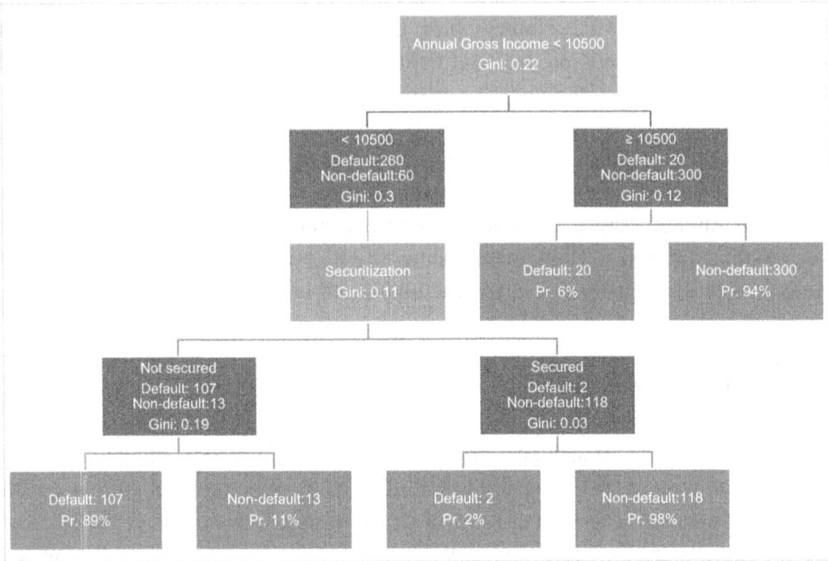

Figure 3.8 Example of a Decision Tree

There are a number of machine learning algorithms employed for the design of decision trees. All of them are used for the assessment of the classification power of parameters and the parameters' cutoff values. For instance, important classifiers can be selected using the Gini impurity coefficient (Equation 3.15).

$$GI = 1 - \sum_{i=1}^{n} (p_i)^2 = 1 - ((PD)^2 + (1 - PD)^2) \qquad (3.15)$$

where:
n = number of classes
PD = probability of default

Gini coefficient is a measurement that shows the probability that the groups were classified incorrectly. Designing a decision tree, a data analyst has to select the parameters with the lowest value of the Gini coefficient to minimize the error of classification.[13] To calculate the Gini coefficient, first of all, default and non-default observations have to be split for each classifier. The next step is to calculate Gini scores of all parameters and select the lowest one as the root node of the tree. To calculate the Gini impurity of a classifier, Gini scores of its "True" and "False" nodes have to be calculated. The final Gini score of the parameter will equal the average value of weighted Gini scores of its nodes. For example, in Figure 3.8, to calculate the Gini coefficient of "Annual gross income < 10500 euro", the following calculation should be applied (Equation 3.16).

$$GI_{\text{annual gross income} < 10500} = \omega_{TRUE} GI_{TRUE} + \omega_{FALSE} GI_{FALSE} = \\ = \frac{320}{640} \times 0.3 + \frac{320}{640} \times 0.12 = 0.22 \qquad (3.16)$$

where:

ω_{TRUE} = the share of "True" node observations in all observations of the root node

ω_{FALSE} = the share of "False" node observations in all observations of the root node

GI_{TRUE} = Gini impurity of the "True" node

GI_{FALSE} = Gini impurity of the "False" node

When an independent variable is categorical and has more than 2 values (e.g. employment: full-time, part-time, unemployed), all possible combinations of its values should be considered as classifiers. When the parameter has a numeric scale (e.g. annual gross income in Figure 3.8), the limit value (e.g. 10500 euro in Figure 3.8) with the highest classification power should be chosen. To select it, all Gini coefficients of the limit values can be calculated in the following way:

1) Sort all borrowers by a continuous independent factor from lowest to highest.
2) Calculate the average values for all neighbor observations of the parameter.
3) Calculate the impurity values for each average value using average values as a separator value for a classifier leaf (e.g. if x < average value).
4) Choose the average value with the lowest Gini coefficient as a separator

As a result, all default and non-default values will be split into "True" and "False" leaf nodes. If the leaves consist of the mixtures of defaults and non-defaults, further separation using another classifier can be required. For each impure leaf, the Gini scores of all classifiers have to be calculated again based on the respective

[13] Raileanu / Stoffel (2004) pp. 77–93

leaves' subsets. The next step is to compare the classifier with the lowest Gini impurity with the impurity of the analyzed node. When the separation by the selected classifier leads to Gini impurity decrease, the leaf should be split by the new classifier. When the True/False node itself has the lowest score, then there is no reason for the further borrower's separation and this node becomes a final leaf. For example, in Figure 3.8, the leaf "annual gross income < 10500 euro" had the Gini impurity at the level of 0.3 and the "securitization" classifier's Gini was 0.11, therefore the tree's node should be extended with this parameter. On another hand, the leaf "annual gross income > 10500 euro" had a lower impurity (0.12) than all other possible classifiers, consequently, it became a leaf node. The secured and not secured nodes had also the lowest possible Gini scores (0.03 and 0.19 respectively), thus, these nodes should be considered as the leaves. To conclude, the procedure of decision tree extension should be repeated for every further node while the nodes' impurity is higher than new separators' Gini scores.

The key advantage of decision trees is their high interpretability of how the model's results were derived. The hierarchical and consistent structure of decision trees allows managers to trace the rationale of the classification. At the same time, this structure allows decision trees to illustrate non-linear relationships between independent and dependent variables. Another benefit of decision tree application is that this method deals well with missing values. On another hand, decision trees have a number of limitations. Firstly, decision trees can be unstable to changes in the training data—it means that little adjustments of the input data can dramatically change the structure of a decision tree.[14] This characteristic influences the high variance of decision trees. Secondly, the decision tree method aims to minimize the classification errors of the local nodes and does not take into account the general classification error of the model.

3.2.3 Random Forest

Random forests are a group of machine learning methods that are employed for classification and regression problems. In credit scoring, random forests can be applied for the classification of defaults and non-defaults events. The design of the random forest model requires building a set of decision trees based on randomly selected training data. As a result, the model classifies default and non-defaults based on a majority of the individual decision trees' classifications. Generally, random forests have higher classification accuracy than decision trees,

[14] Friedman et al. (2001) p. 312

because the aggregation of multiple random decision trees reduces the model's variance and prevents the model from overfitting.[15] After the construction of many decision trees, a random forest algorithm makes new classifications based on the aggregated results of all trees (Figure 3.9). For instance, if there are 500 trees in the random forest model: 450 trees classified a new borrower as defaulted and 50 trees classified the borrower as non-defaulted, based on the majority of trees, the model will classify the borrower as potentially defaulted.

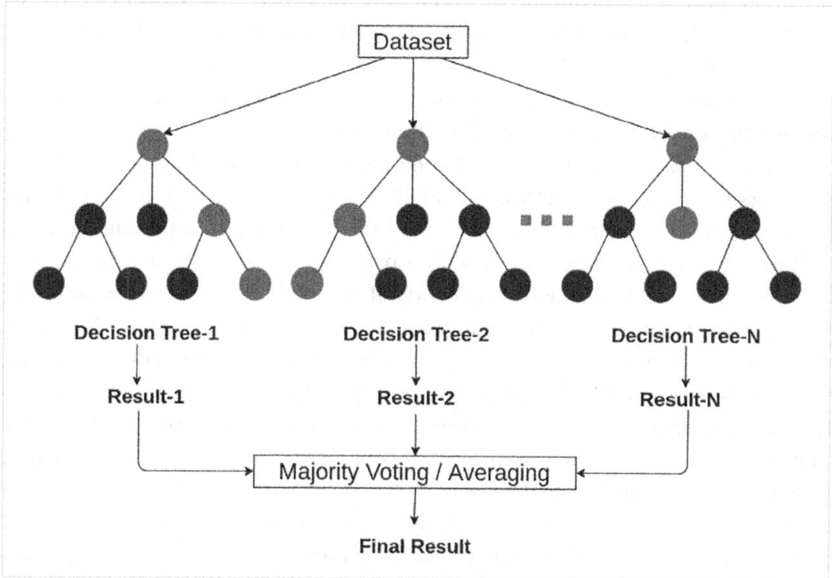

Figure 3.9 Example of Random Forest Structure[16]

The key concept of random forests is to construct multiple decision trees that will be uncorrelated between each other. A big number of independent trees will allow the model to consider different possible combinations of features and training datasets, consequently, the model will be more robust in processing new data. To ensure that the decision trees will be uncorrelated, the random forest algorithm uses such techniques as bootstrap aggregation (Bagging) and random feature selection. The bootstrapping mechanism is a random sampling of the

[15] Ali et al. (2012) p. 273

[16] Sharma (2020) p. 2

subset of training data with replacement. Typically, the size of the bootstrapped dataset is about two-thirds of the size of the training data.[17] Unselected part of the training data is called the Out-Of-Bag sample. The Out-Of-Bag sample can be used for further validation of the model's results measuring the proportion of correctly classified observations. The replacement characteristic means that randomly selected observations from the original dataset can be duplicated in a decision tree's subsample. Usage of duplicates in the subsample can decrease the "outliers" error. If a decision tree is based on the unbalanced training dataset, some rare groups of borrowers can be misclassified. The replacement method can repeat these rare classes multiple times in bootstrap samples that will increase the weights of these groups. To summarize, the bagging technique allows the model to generate multiple diverse data samples based on one training dataset and design the number of decision trees based on these samples.

Random feature selection is the second method that is used by random forests to diversify the decision trees. Within this approach, not all parameters are employed in decision tree training. Each of the decision trees of a random forest will be built on a training sample with a part of randomly selected independent variables. As a result, the random selection of the model's parameters prevents the model from overemphasizing certain parameters and neglecting others. Moreover, decision trees will have different sets of selected features which will decrease the correlation between trees.[18] Typically, for classification problems, the number of randomly selected features for decision trees equals the square root of the overall number of model parameters. However, this number, as well as the bootstrapping size, can be adjusted by the analyst.

A big number of diverse decision trees, with different structures and selected features, makes it difficult to explain the importance of the parameters. An individual decision tree allows one to trace the classification process and observe the logics of separators. Considering the fact that the standard size of a random forest model is around 500 decision trees, the visualization and interpretation of such an amount of trees become inconvenient. Therefore, other methods for parameters importance analysis should be applied.

Many post-hoc variable analyses can be applied for random forests. One of the approaches is to test a decrease of the model's accuracy with and without each of the parameters. In this case, an original model is used as a benchmark. In the next step, input data of a model's variable is randomly shuffled. After it,

---

[17] Efron / Tibshirani (1997) pp. 548–560

[18] Ibrahim (2019) pp. 774–798

the random forest has to be retrained with all previous parameters and the shuffled variable instead of the original one. The following decrease/increase in the model's accuracy demonstrates the impact of the parameter. The higher decrease of accuracy means the bigger importance of the variable. The data shuffling and accuracy checks procedures have to be repeated for each variable separately. The limitation of this method consists of the fact that it does not explain whether a parameter has a positive or negative impact.

Another variables importance analysis is based on Gini coefficients. Separators in decision trees decrease the Gini-impurity of the trees. Therefore, all reductions of Gini-impurities by each variable in every decision tree of a random forest can be aggregated and assigned to the respective variables. The variable with the biggest aggregated reduction of Gini-impurity will have the biggest model's importance and vice versa.

The random forest method has several advantages and disadvantages. The ensemble approach of random forests allows to decrease the variance of the individual decision trees and prevent the model from overfitting. Another advantage of a random forest is that it can handle missing values. Moreover, a random forest technique does not require prelaminar normalization of variables or feature selection. The biggest limitation of this approach is the low interpretability. Features importance analysis becomes more complicated due to a big number of random trees. Another limitation of random forest is that it requires a lot of computation power because of the construction of many trees.

3.3 Methods of Model Validation

Model validation is a process of assessment of the model's statistical performance. Validation of machine learning models usually requires splitting all data into training and testing datasets. In supervised learning, the training dataset consists of independent variables and a labeled dependent variable. During learning, supervised AI models use dependent variable labels as a benchmark which they need to fit. Internal validation allows an analyst to test the model's accuracy based on the training sample.[19] For example, residual analysis allows one to see the difference between predicted and actual values of the training dataset. The testing dataset consists of a sample that was not employed during the model design process. A trained model uses features inputs of a testing dataset to make

[19] Steyerberg et al. (2001) pp. 774–776

predictions. Finally, the created predictions have to be compared to actual values of the dependent variable of the testing dataset.

At the stage of validation, a set of criteria, tools, and procedures is used to assess the quality of the designed models. Two of the most frequent measures of the model's quality in forecasting problems are Mean Squared Error (MSE) and Mean Absolute Error (MAE). MSE penalizes models more for big deviations of prediction from actual values than MAE. That makes MSE more sensitive to model errors compared to MAE. MSE and MAE can be represented in the following way (Equation 3.17 and Equation 3.18).

$$MSE = \frac{1}{N}\sum_{i=1}^{N}(d_i - y_i)^2 \tag{3.17}$$

$$MAE = \frac{1}{N}\sum_{i=1}^{N}|d_i - y_i| \tag{3.18}$$

where:
N = number of observations
d = actual value of i-th observation
y = predicted value of i-th observation

MSE and MAE are good tools to measure the model's error using absolute metrics. These tools can be used to compare the performance of different models, which use the same data. However, these methods do not explain the level of the model's accuracy and cannot be used for comparison of models that employ different data. In these cases, data analysts should apply relative measures instead of MSE and MAE. R-squared is a relative measure that is used for model's accuracy of linear regression models (Equation 3.19).

$$R^2 = 1 - \frac{\sum_{i=1}^{N}(d_i - y_i)^2}{\sum_{i=1}^{N}(\bar{y} - y_i)^2} \tag{3.19}$$

where:
$\bar{y} = \frac{1}{N}\sum_{i=1}^{N} y_i$ = mean value of the independent variable

R-squared measure equal to the proportion of the dependent variable's variance explained by the predictors to the total variance of the independent variable. R-squared values can be in a range from 0 to 1. A Higher R-squared value means higher prediction accuracy of the model. For example, when the R-squared value is close to 0, it means that the model has a bad fit; when the R-squared value is close to 1, the model has high prediction performance.

Similar to R-squared, a number of pseudo-R-squared can be applied in logistic models. Efron's, McFadden's, Cox / Snell, McKelvey / Zavoina's, and Nagelkerke / Cragg / Uhler's are the most popular pseudo-R-squared models. For example, McFadden's pseudo-R squared is based on the maximum likelihood of the model (Equation 3.20).

$$R^2_{\text{McFadden}} = 1 - \frac{\log(L_c)}{\log(L_{\text{null}})} \tag{3.20}$$

where:
L_c = the maximum likelihood of the current model
L_{null} = the maximum likelihood of the model with only an intercept and no covariates

Out-of-bag error is a tool of internal validation of random forest models. It was mentioned earlier that the bootstrapping method selects randomly a part of the observations for the model training. The rest of the observations, which were not included in bootstrap datasets, can be used for testing purposes. The trained random forest model can make predictions to the out-of-bag dataset and compare them to the actual values of the out-of-bag sample. Then, the out-of-bag error equals the proportion of misclassified observations to the overall number of out-of-bag observations. This measure is frequently applied to test the model's performance and compare different random forest models between each other.

One of the most effective ways to evaluate the accuracy of a classification model based on the testing dataset is to analyze the confusion matrix. In credit scoring modeling, default and non-default events may be binary represented as 1 and 0 respectively. Then confusion matrix will consist of the following elements:

- True positive (TP): Prediction is default (1) and actual value is default (1)
- True negative (TN): Prediction is non-default (0) and actual value is non-default (0)
- False positive (FP): Prediction is default (1) and actual value is non-default (0)
- False negative (FN): Prediction is non-default (0) and actual value is default (1)

True positive and true negative values stand for correctly classified defaults and non-defaults events respectively. False positive values create false alarms—credit-worthy clients are classified as distressed. False negative classifications influence unexpected credit risks because default borrowers are not identified.

The accuracy ratio evaluates the proportion of the correctly classified observations to all observations (Equation 3.21).

$$\text{Accuracy} = \frac{\text{TP} + \text{TN}}{\text{TP} + \text{FP} + \text{FN} + \text{TN}} \tag{3.21}$$

In credit scoring, the sensitivity ratio is one of the most important validation tools, because it shows the share of correctly classified defaults to the all actual defaults of the testing data (Equation 3.22).

$$\text{Sensitivity} = \frac{\text{TP}}{\text{TP} + \text{FN}} \tag{3.22}$$

The precision metric is another ratio that analyzes the correctness of default classifications. Precision equals the proportion of correctly classified defaults to all predictions which were classified as defaults (Equation 3.23).

$$\text{Precision} = \frac{\text{TP}}{\text{TP} + \text{FP}} \tag{3.23}$$

F1-score is another accuracy metric that equals the weighted average of sensitivity and precision metrics (Equation 3.24).

$$F_1 = 2 \cdot \frac{\text{precision} \cdot \text{sensitivity}}{\text{precision} + \text{sensitivity}} = \frac{\text{TP}}{\text{TP} + \frac{1}{2}(\text{FP} + \text{FN})} \tag{3.24}$$

Generally, the outcomes of logistic and tree-based credit scoring models are represented as probabilities of defaults and have values between 0 and 1. To convert the continuous numeric value in a binary output, a certain threshold has to be applied. For example, if PD equals to or more than 0.5, then the value is classified as 1 (default); if PD is smaller than 0.5, then output is classified as 0 (non-default). However, to select a threshold with the lowest number of misclassified outcomes, Receiver Operating Characteristic (ROC) curve can be applied. The ROC curve illustrates the dependence of the share of correctly classified defaults on the share of incorrectly classified non-defaults regarding threshold settings. Graphically, the ROC curve can be represented on the plot with sensitivity and false positive rate axes. The false positive rate can be calculated using the following formula (Equation 3.25).

$$\text{False Positive Rate} = \frac{\text{FP}}{\text{FP} + \text{TN}} \tag{3.25}$$

Based on the ROC curve plot, Area under Curve (AUC) can be evaluated. The AUC score is applied for the comparison of different models between each other. The value of the AUC parameter varies from 0.5 to 1. A higher AUC value means that the model has better quality and vice versa.

Empirical Analysis 4

4.1 Data Analysis

To compare the efficiency of random forest, decision trees, and logit methods in credit scoring, all the models will be trained on the individuals' banking-related data. The dataset is anonymized and provided by organization X. The dataset consists of transactional data with economic and social-demographic features of retail-banking customers. The default statuses of individuals are composed of "1" and "0" values, where "1" stands for the default status within the last 12 months, and "0" stands for non-default status within the same period. The original dataset consists of 99,628 observations, 758 independent variables, and 1 dependent variable. Independent variables include both categorical and numerical features. The provided dataset is cleaned from missing values and has only complete cases. Every observation of the dataset is independent of other observations.

The data consists of 9,416 (9.5%) default events and 90,212 (90.5%) non-default events. The dataset has imbalanced data with a low amount of default events. The models, which are trained on the imbalanced data, tend to classify all observations as the majority class (non-default). As a result, usage of the imbalanced data can decrease the performance results of the models.[1] To create a dataset with balanced groups, several techniques can be applied. This research employs the undersampling method. The goal of the undersampling method is to shrink the majority class observations and reach a balanced distribution of classes. Instead of using over ninety-thousands of non-default observations, the undersampling algorithm randomly selected around 15 percent of non-default events (13,531 observations). The final dataset, which will be used for the next

[1] He / Garcia (2009) pp. 11–33

B. Popovych, *Application of AI in Credit Scoring Modeling*, BestMasters,
https://doi.org/10.1007/978-3-658-40180-1_4

analysis, consists of 22,947 observations, where 9,416 (41%) observations are defaults and 13,531 (59%) observations are non-defaults.

According to the assumptions of the logit model, the multicollinearity of independent variables has to be reduced. Based on the Pearson correlation analysis, 6,486 pairs of numerical features have a high correlation (higher than 0.9 or lower than −0.9). There are several ways to reduce multicollinearity. For instance, analysis of Variance Inflation Factors (VIFs) can help to detect model features that cause high multicollinearity. VIF evaluates the increase of variance of an estimated model parameter when parameters are correlated.[2] Identifying parameters with high VIF values and removing them may require training a number of models. Considering the high amount of variables in the dataset, this method may be time-consuming and inconvenient to apply. Another method of dealing with multicollinearity is Principal Component Analysis (PCA). The goal of PCA is to reduce the number of correlated variables to a set of less correlated principal components reducing the dimensionality of the model. Due to the linear combination of the correlated variables, principal components maintain the most information of the reduced variables.[3] The limitation of the PCA method is that model independent variables become less interpretable. The Least Absolute Shrinkage and Selection Operator (LASSO) regression is another tool that can help one to deal with multicollinearity. Application of LASSO regression allows one to automatically reduce most of the parameters penalizing their size.[4] Within LASSO regression, the weights of less important parameters go to zero. As result, the LASSO model automatically selects a set of parameters that are less sensitive to multicollinearity and can be used for further training of the logit model. Mathematically, LASSO simultaneously minimizes the difference between predicted and actual values and a sum of parameter weights. Its loss function can be represented as the following equation (Equation 4.1).

$$\sum_{i=0}^{M} (y_i - \hat{y}_i)^2 = \sum_{i=1}^{M} \left(y_i - \sum_{j=0}^{p} w_j \times x_{ij}\right) + \lambda \sum_{j=0}^{p} |w_j| \quad (4.1)$$

where:
y_i = actual dependent value of i_{th} observation
$\hat{y}_i$ = estimated dependent value of i_{th} observation
w_j = weight of j_{th} parameter
M = number of observations

[2] Akinwande et al. (2015) pp. 2–5
[3] Perez (2017) p. 15
[4] Chong / Jun (2005) p. 104

λ = penalty strength parameter

To train and validate LASSO and all following models, the data was split into training and test datasets. The size of training data is 16,062 observations (70%). The test dataset consists of 6,885 observations (30%). All numerical independent variables were standardized. As a result of data standardization, all numerical parameters have a mean of 0 and a standard deviation of 1. The applied LASSO model selected the 13 most important parameters from 758 independent parameters of the original dataset (Figure 4.1).

Figure 4.1 is composed of frequency plots of the selected numerical variables. Some of the variables have extreme outliers. For example, V190 is highly skewed to the left. Since all variables are centered, most observations of V190 are distributed around 0 (median = −0.2627, mean = 0) (Table 4.1). The minimum value for V190 is close to 0 and is equal to −1.1990, while the maximum value equals 11.8874, indicating positive outliers. V365 is highly skewed to the right and has extreme negative outliers (minimum = −50.7361, maximum = 0.3036). V371 and V757 are examples of unbalanced variables. V371 has 9 unique values, where the value "0.0357" has 91% frequency. The huge concentration of V371 observations is also confirmed by the same values of the 1st, 2nd, and 3rd quartiles, which are equal to 0.0357. Despite the low number of unique values, V371 has a big range (minimum = −8.3999, maximum = 8.4712). V757 has 10 unique data entries where the 2nd and 3rd quartiles are equal to 0.4550. The negative result of the employment of the imbalanced predictors is that they can lead to overfitting of the model.

Table 4.1 Independent Variables Descriptive Statistics

	Min.	1st Qu.	Median	Mean	3rd Qu.	Max.
V190	−1.1990	−0.6826	−0.2627	0.0000	0.3826	11.8874
V270	−8.4762	−0.4393	0.1347	0.0000	0.7088	1.5699
V273	−7.8578	−0.5460	0.0633	0.0000	0.4695	2.2975
V275	−3.1665	−0.7076	−0.0519	0.0000	0.4398	7.8164
V291	−2.5933	−0.8247	−0.4402	0.0000	0.5979	6.7880
V297	−3.9703	−0.8886	−0.2186	0.0000	0.7193	7.2848

(continued)

Table 4.1 (continued)

	Min.	1st Qu.	Median	Mean	3rd Qu.	Max.
V365	−50.7361	0.0089	0.1661	0.0000	0.2727	0.3036
V371	−8.3999	0.0357	0.0357	0.0000	0.0357	8.4712
V415	−5.5211	−0.5641	0.0079	0.0000	0.7705	2.1051
V560	−2.2437	−0.7878	−0.0731	0.0000	0.7210	2.6269
V740	−2.5971	−0.6916	−0.0845	0.0000	0.6130	6.0938
V750	−2.4952	−0.8279	0.0058	0.0000	0.5616	8.0647
V757	−4.3508	−0.1457	0.4550	0.0000	0.4550	1.6565

Figure 4.2 illustrates the frequencies of default (pink color) and non-default (light-blue color) classes for every predictor. Based on the plots, the ability of each variable to separate the dependent variable was preliminary analyzed. For example, a majority of defaults have lower V560 values than a majority of non-defaults. Based on Table 4.2 and Table 4.3, the absolute difference between V560 means of default and non-default groups equals 0.46. In addition, V365 could be another possible classifier. For V365, the absolute difference between default and non-default groups means is 0.45. Besides, 75% of default V365 observations are equal to or lower than 0.10 (3rd quartile). At the same time, 75% of its non-default events are equal to or higher than 0.20 (1st quartile). Therefore, default borrowers tend to have lower values of V365 than non-default ones. For V190, the absolute difference between means of default and non-default classes is 0.41. Moreover, 75% of default V190 observations are equal or lower than 0.06 (3rd quartile) and 50% of its non-default events are equal or higher than 0.17 (2nd quartile). Thus, non-default borrowers tend to have higher values of V365 than default ones. It is important to note that means comparison does not take into account the overlaps of variances of the default and non-default classes. Furthermore, descriptive statistics of individual parameters do not illustrate possible linear and non-linear combinations between them, which can improve classification performance. Therefore, the classification power of independent variables has to be analyzed based on the following multivariate models.

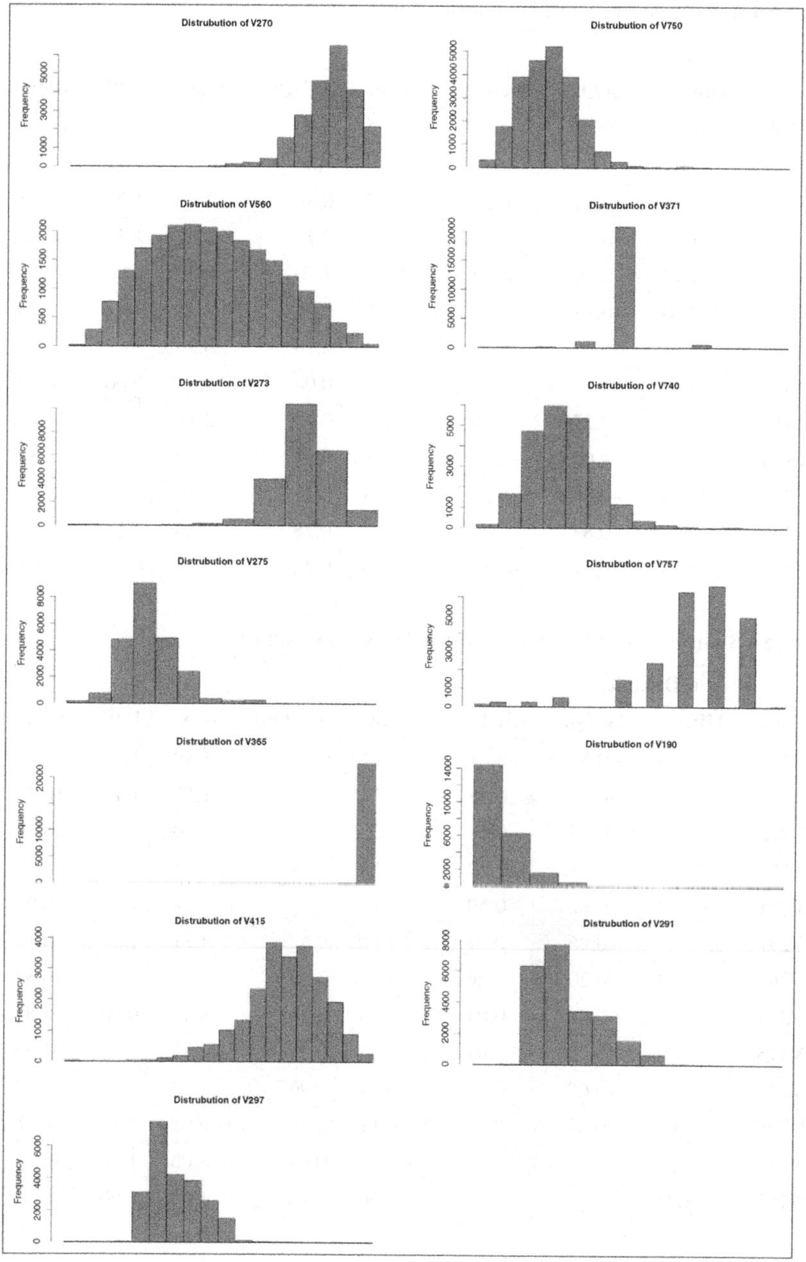

Figure 4.1 Frequency Distribution of Variables

Table 4.2 Independent Variables Statistics for Default Class

	Default							
Coef.	**Min.**	**1st Qu.**	**Median**	**Mean**	**3rd Qu.**	**Max.**	**IQR**	**Range**
V190	−1.20	−0.78	−0.44	−0.24	0.06	10.86	0.84	12.06
V270	−7.04	−0.44	0.42	0.15	1.00	1.57	1.44	8.61
V273	−7.86	−0.34	0.27	0.15	0.88	2.30	1.22	10.16
V275	−3.17	−0.54	0.11	0.16	0.77	7.82	1.31	10.98
V291	−2.59	−0.79	−0.32	0.15	1.10	6.79	1.88	9.38
V297	−2.60	−0.82	−0.08	0.15	0.85	7.28	1.67	9.88
V365	−50.74	−0.17	0.01	−0.27	0.10	0.28	0.27	51.01
V371	−6.29	0.04	0.04	0.08	0.04	8.47	0.00	14.76
V415	−4.57	−0.37	0.20	0.19	0.77	2.11	1.14	6.67
V560	−2.24	−1.00	−0.36	−0.27	0.35	2.57	1.35	4.82
V740	−2.41	−0.84	−0.24	−0.16	0.45	6.09	1.29	8.51
V750	−2.22	−0.83	−0.27	−0.18	0.28	8.06	1.11	10.28
V757	−4.35	−0.15	−0.15	0.00	0.46	1.66	0.60	6.01

Table 4.3 Independent Variables Statistics for Non-Default Class

	Non-Default							
Coef.	**Min.**	**1st Qu.**	**Median**	**Mean**	**3rd Qu.**	**Max.**	**IQR**	**Range**
V190	−1.20	−0.59	−0.11	0.17	0.61	11.89	1.21	13.09
V270	−8.48	−0.73	0.13	−0.11	0.42	1.57	1.15	10.05
V273	−7.86	−0.55	−0.14	−0.11	0.47	2.30	1.02	10.16
V275	−3.17	−0.71	−0.22	−0.11	0.28	7.82	0.98	10.98
V291	−2.52	−0.82	−0.59	−0.10	0.33	4.44	1.15	6.96
V297	−3.97	−0.96	−0.39	−0.11	0.62	4.81	1.57	8.78
V365	−26.53	0.20	0.26	0.19	0.29	0.30	0.09	26.83
V371	−8.40	0.04	0.04	−0.06	0.04	8.47	0.00	16.87
V415	−5.52	−0.75	0.01	−0.13	0.58	2.11	1.33	7.63
V560	−2.19	−0.60	0.17	0.19	0.96	2.63	1.56	4.82
V740	−2.60	−0.62	0.04	0.11	0.70	6.09	1.32	8.69
V750	−2.50	−0.55	0.01	0.13	0.84	8.06	1.39	10.56
V757	−4.35	−0.15	0.46	0.00	0.46	1.66	0.60	6.01

To analyze the linear relationships between the independent variables, a correlation matrix was calculated (Figure 4.3). The correlation matrix consists of correlation values of each pair of independent variables. As all variables are continuous, the Pearson correlation metric was applied. All correlation values are in a range from -1 to $+1$, where -1 stands for negative correlation (red color), 0 indicates absence of correlation (white color), and $+1$ is an indicator of positive correlation (blue color). Most independent variables have a low or moderate correlation. However, the pairs V270-V273, V273-V275, and V270-V275 have high positive correlation values: 0.91, 0.93, and 0.88 respectively. The V371 variable has the lowest correlation with other parameters. This can be a consequence of the low amount of the variable's extremely imbalanced values.

4.2 Logistic Regression

4.2.1 Model Description

The logit model is a traditional credit scoring model that will be used as a benchmark for AI models. To develop a reliable logit model, its assumptions should be met. The first assumption of the logit model is that all observations should be independent of each other. An example of dependent data records would be when different observations describe default events of the same borrower over several periods. Based on the data provider information all observations are independent of each other. Another important assumption is about the low multicollinearity of independent variables. LASSO regression helped to select the most important variables and penalized less important variables. However, there is no guarantee that the logit built on the selected variables will have no multicollinearity. For instance, the analysis of the correlation matrix showed that there are pairs of variables with high correlation. To identify and exclude the parameters that increase multicollinearity, the VIF method will be applied. Variance Inflation Factor can be calculated using the following equation (Equation 4.2).

$$VIF_i = \frac{1}{1 - R_i^2} \tag{4.2}$$

where:
$R_i^2 = R^2$ of the regression of i_{th} parameter on the remaining parameters

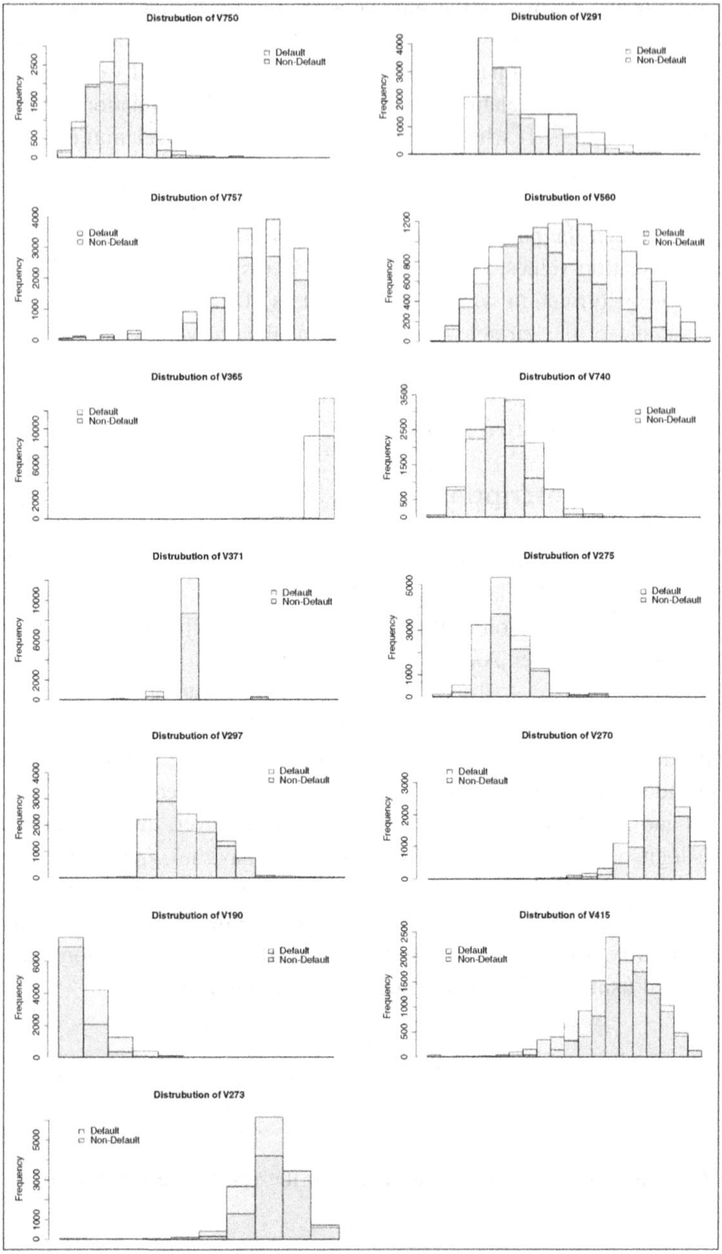

Figure 4.2 Frequency Distribution of Defaults and Non-Defaults by Variables

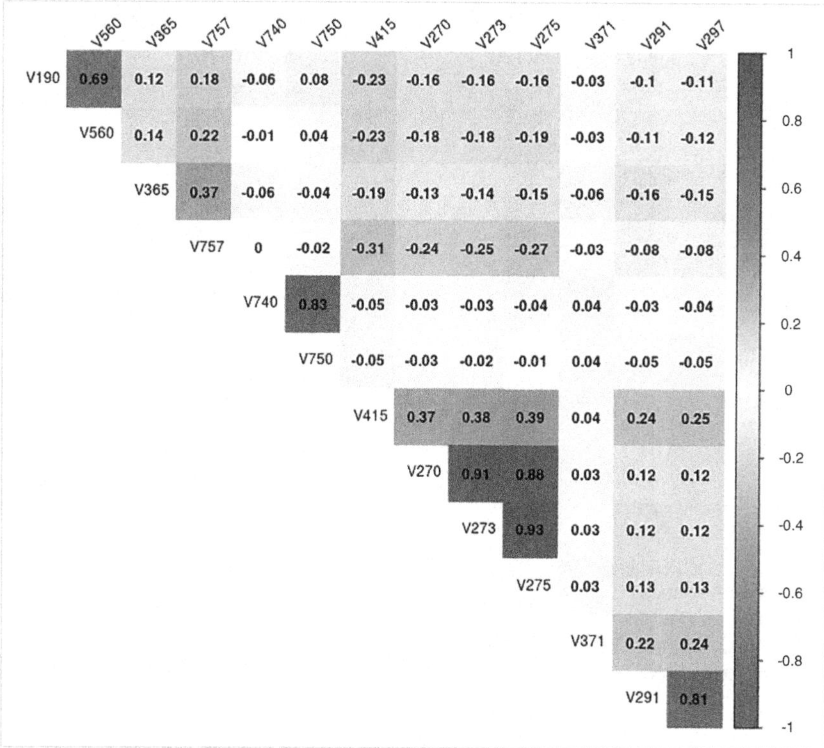

Figure 4.3 Correlation Matrix of Independent Variables

Table 4.4 illustrates that the majority of variables have low VIF values. However, V275 and V273 have high values of VIF: 8.3 and 11.3 respectively. To reduce multicollinearity, V273 with the highest VIF will be excluded and the logit model will be retrained again. VIF values of the retrained model are lower than 5 (Table 4.5), consequently, the multicollinearity assumption is met.

4.2.2 Model Interpretation

The final logit model consists of 12 numerical parameters. Table 4.6 illustrates that V270, V275, V297, and V415 are not statistically significant ($P > 0.05$). All other variables can be considered statistically significant ($P < 0.05$). Due to

Table 4.4 Variance Inflation Factor of Independent Variables

Variable	VIF
V190	2.037634
V270	6.346231
V273	11.280856
V275	8.283661
V291	2.925436
V297	2.875588
V365	1.993984
V371	1.079584
V415	1.284392
V560	1.970268
V740	3.134110
V750	2.986783
V757	1.904076

Table 4.5 Variance Inflation Factor of Independent Variables of the Final Logit Model

Variable	VIF
V190	2.037530
V270	4.431783
V275	4.547916
V291	2.924926
V297	2.874688
V365	1.993904
V371	1.079585
V415	1.284591
V560	1.970240
V740	3.123803
V750	2.975032
V757	1.903516

standardized values of independent variables, weights of the parameters can be compared and used as indicators of variables' importance. V365 has the strongest impact on the probability of default (weight = −8.36). An increase of V365 influences a PD decrease. V757 is another variable with a high impact on the

PD (weight = 1.69). An increase of V757 causes an increase in PD. All other parameters are weaker classifiers because they have low importance (absolute weights < 1).

Table 4.6 Coefficients of the Logit Model

Variable	Weight	S.E.	Wald Z	Pr(>|Z|)
Intercept	0.0687	0.0256	2.68	0.0073
V190	−0.1571	0.0326	−4.82	<0.0001
V270	0.0783	0.0440	1.78	0.0751
V275	0.0508	0.0447	1.14	0.2555
V291	−0.2922	0.0353	−8.29	<0.0001
V297	−0.0581	0.0350	−1.66	0.0965
V365	−8.3604	0.1664	−50.24	<0.0001
V371	0.1846	0.0221	8.35	<0.0001
V415	0.0018	0.0240	0.07	0.9412
V560	−0.2928	0.0298	−9.82	<0.0001
V740	−0.5398	0.0410	−13.16	<0.0001
V750	0.0857	0.0402	2.13	0.0328
V757	1.6928	0.0417	40.58	<0.0001

4.2.3 Model Performance

To analyze the model performance, in sample and out-of-sample validations were applied. The in-sample validation requires the training dataset to access the model classification accuracy. For the out-of-sample validation, the testing dataset was employed. The output probabilities of the logit model were transformed to the binary outputs (0, 1) for further validation analysis. For instance, all output values that are higher than 0.5 are classified as defaults (1), all outputs that are equal to or lower than 0.5 were classified as non-defaults (0). In the confusion matrix for the training data (Table 4.7), the proportion of misclassified defaults (7.17%) is higher than the proportion of misclassified non-default (5.00%). Similarly, the out-of-sample validation illustrates that there are more misclassified defaults (6.70%) than misclassified non-default (4.91%). Thus, the logit model has a higher ability to detect non-default borrowers than default ones (Table 4.8).

Table 4.7 Confusion Matrix for In-Sample Classification of the Logit Model

	Actual non-default	Actual default
Predicted non-default	8649	1152
Predicted default	803	5458

Table 4.8 Confusion Matrix for Out-Of-Sample Classification of the Logit Model

	Actual non-default	Actual default
Predicted non-default	3741	461
Predicted default	338	2345

Based on the confusion matrices, the performance metrics of the logit model were estimated (Table 4.9). The validation results show that the model has high classification accuracy both in and out of training samples. For instance, the model classified the testing observations with 88.4% accuracy. At the same time, the sensitivity to the default values is lower than the average accuracy (83.57% for out-of-sample). F1-score, which represents the model's ability to classify defaults, is equal to 0.8544 for the testing dataset. Based on the ROC curve plot for the out-of-sample classification, AUC metric was assessed (Figure 4.4). The high value of the model's AUC (0.9416) implies that the model has a strong ability to distinguish between default and non-default classes.

Table 4.9 Performance Metrics of the Logit Model

In-Sample Validation	Out-Of-Sample Validation
Accuracy: 0.8783 Sensitivity: 0.8257 Precision: 0.8717 F1-score: 0.8481	Accuracy: 0.8840 Sensitivity: 0.8357 Precision: 0.8740 F1-score: 0.8544

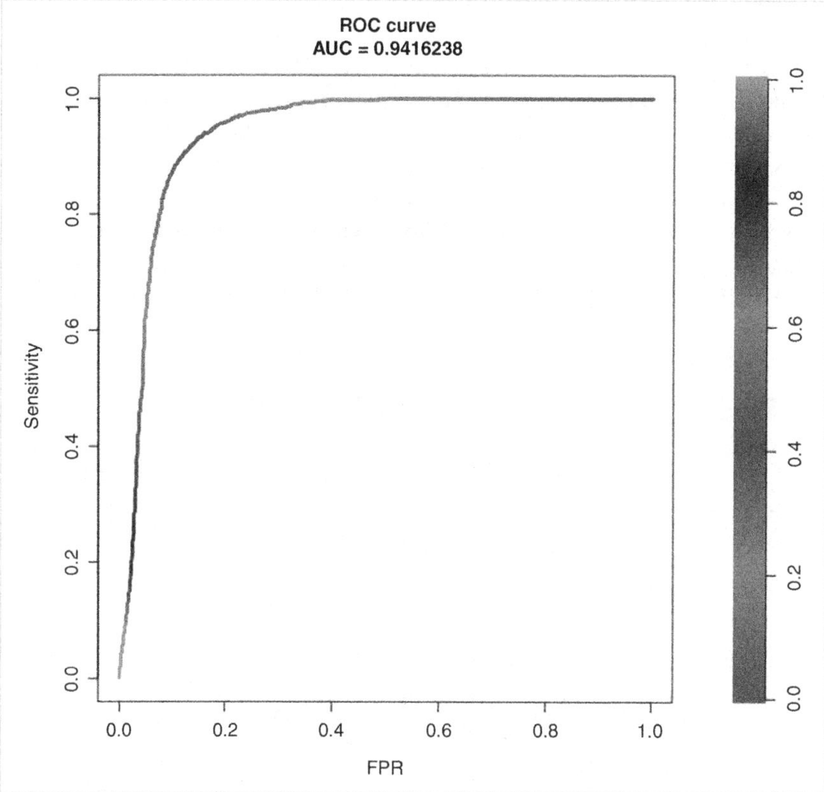

Figure 4.4 ROC Curve for Out-Of-Sample Classification of the Logit Model

4.3 Decision Tree

4.3.1 Model Description and Interpretation

A decision tree is a non-linear machine learning model that was applied for the classification of defaults and non-defaults (Figure 4.5). The decision tree was trained on the 13 independent variables (Figure 4.1). Each inner node of the tree minimizes the impurity of classification. In Figure 4.5, every node splits observation into "True" (left-side leaves) and "False" (right-side leaves) groups. The leaves of the tree are the model's predictions, which represent the probabilities of default. The root node of the tree is V365. V365 is also the most frequent separator of the decision tree. It implies that V365 is the most important classifier because it has the lowest Gini impurity score. V757 and V291 are the other decision tree separators with high classification power. In the longest separators' sequences, the decision tree involves up to 4 nodes. Based on the analysis of nodes' Gini impurities, the impact of the independent variables on the dependent variable can be identified. The increase of V365 and V291 influences the decrease of PD. For example, when V365 is equal to or higher than 0.1747, the estimated PD is equal to 1.78%. The borrowers with higher values of V757 tend to have higher PDs.

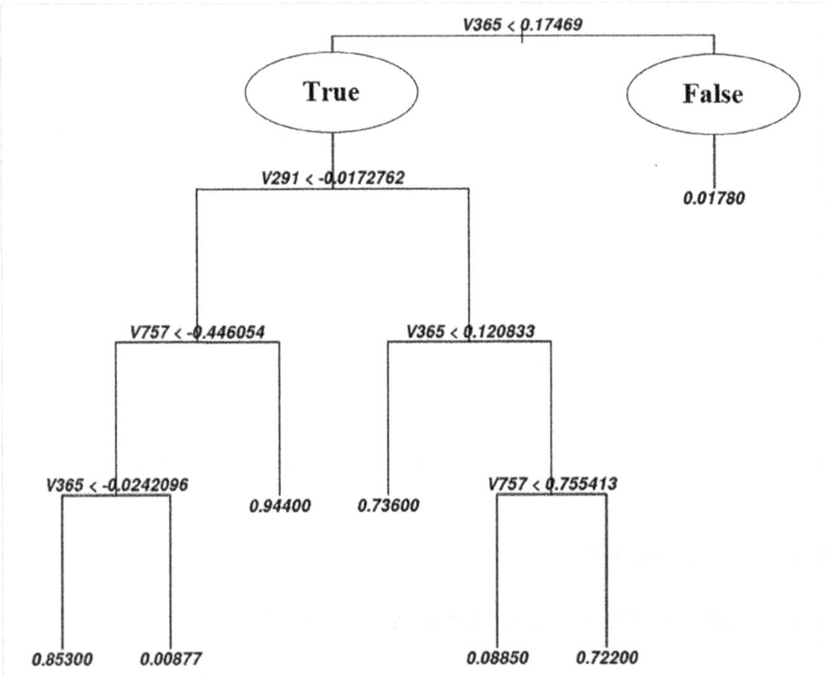

Figure 4.5 Structure of the Decision Tree Model

4.3.2 Model Performance

For the in-sample and out-sample validations of the decision tree model, confusion matrices were developed (Table 4.10 and Table 4.11). In order to build confusion matrices, all probabilities of defaults were converted to 0 (non-default) and 1 (default) based on the cutoff value that is equal to 0.5. Both confusion matrices illustrate that the number of correctly classified observations is significantly higher than the number of incorrectly classified events. Moreover, the decision tree model is more sensitive in the classification of defaults compared to non-defaults. For the in-sample validation, the proportion of misclassified default borrowers is 1.11%, while the share of misclassified non-default borrowers is 8.27%. In the out-of-sample validation, the proportion of misclassified non-default events (8.06%) is also significantly higher than the proportion of misclassified default events (1.26%).

Table 4.10 Confusion Matrix for In-Sample Classification of the Decision Tree Model

	Actual non-default	Actual default
Predicted non-default	8124	178
Predicted default	1328	6432

Table 4.11 Confusion Matrix for Out-Of-Sample Classification of the Decision Tree Model

	Actual non-default	Actual default
Predicted non-default	3524	87
Predicted default	555	2719

Table 4.12 illustrates the performance ratios of the decision tree model. Around 90% of all observations were classified correctly for both training and testing datasets. The model has a high sensitivity level (nearly 97%). However, the sensitivity and F1 scores of the out-of-sample validation (0.9690 and 0.8944, respectively) are slightly lower than the sensitivity and F1 scores of the in-sample test (0.9731 and 0.8952, respectively). Although decision tree models have a risk of overfitting, which results in low performance based on the new data, the applied model has similar results for both in-sample and out-of-sample classifications.

To illustrate the dependence of the share of correctly classified defaults on the share of incorrectly classified non-defaults, the ROC curve was built (Figure 4.6). Area under Curve for the out-of-sample classifications of the decision tree model is equal to 0.9396. To summarize, all analyzed metrics demonstrate that the decision tree model has a good fit and high classification performance.

Table 4.12 Performance Metrics of the Decision Tree Model

In-Sample Validation	Out-Of-Sample Validation
Accuracy: 0.9062 Sensitivity: 0.9731 Precision: 0.8289 F1-score: 0.8952	Accuracy: 0.9068 Sensitivity: 0.9690 Precision: 0.8305 F1-score: 0.8944

4.4 Random Forest

4.4.1 Model Description

Random forest is another machine learning technique that is applied in this research for the assessment of PDs of borrowers. The random forest model is based on the aggregated results of multiple decision trees, which are trained on the randomly selected subsamples. In this research, the random forest algorithm used the results of 500 trees. The model is trained on the 13 independent variables, which are described previously (Table 4.1). Each decision tree was built on a dataset with 3 randomly selected independent variables. Using the bootstrapping method, each tree is based on a sample of randomly selected observations with replacement. The size of the trees datasets is equal to 10152 observations (63.2% of the size of the training dataset).

4.4.2 Model Interpretation

To assess the variables' importance of the random forest model, average values of Gini decreased for every separator were estimated (Figure 4.7). The separators which decrease Gini impurity more than others have higher classification importance. V365 is the dominant classifier of the random forest model. V757, V560, and V291 are other important separators of the model. However, in comparison to V365, all other variables have considerably low importance. For instance, V365

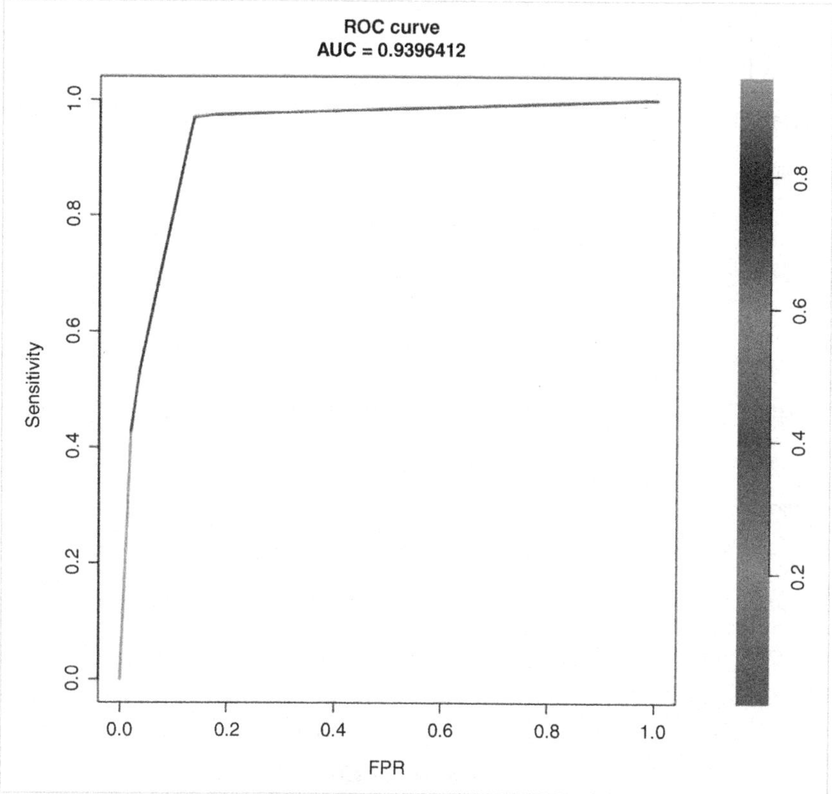

Figure 4.6 ROC Curve for Out-Of-Sample Classification of the Decision Tree Model

decreased the Gini impurity of all trees on average by 4930, while the values of the average Gini decrease for V757, V560, and V291 were 386, 342, and 341, respectively. It is important to mention, analysis of the Gini decrease has its limitations. First, this method does not indicate the direction of impact of the parameter. It is unclear whether parameters increase or decrease the PDs of borrowers. Second, the Gini decrease score is a metric that can be applied only for a relative comparison of the parameters between each other. It does not explain the degree of impact on the dependent variable.

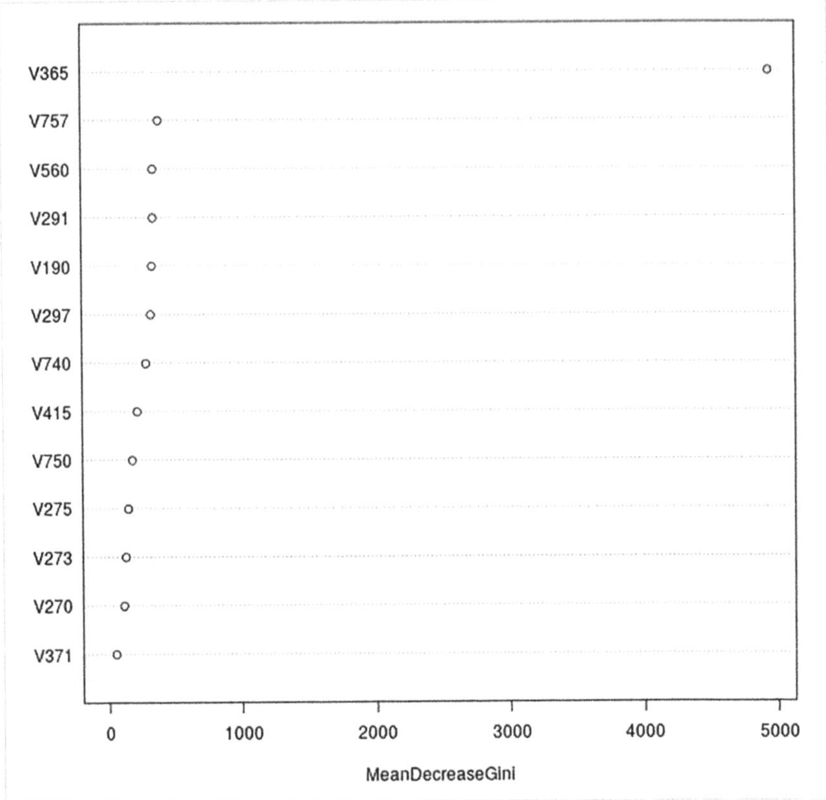

Figure 4.7 Importance of Features of the Random Forest Model

In order to avoid the limitations of the Gini decrease score and explain the impact of the parameters of the random forest, the methods of local interpretation can be applied. The local interpretation techniques assess the features' influence on a specific prediction. In this research, Local Interpretable Model-agnostic Explanations (LIME) will be applied for the local interpretation of the independent variables. LIME is a method that can be used for local interpretation of black-box models, creating simpler, more interpretable models (e.g. linear models).[5] Although the linear model may be weak in the global explanation of nonlinear patterns, it can illustrate the linear relationships of parameters based on

[5] Ribeiro et al. (2016) pp. 1135

the local neighborhoods of individual observations. Such linear local model can be represented as the following equation (Equation 4.3) (Figure 4.8).

$$g(z') = w_g \cdot z' \quad (4.3)$$

where:
z' = sample of observations from the training data around an individual prediction
w_g = local weights of independent variables

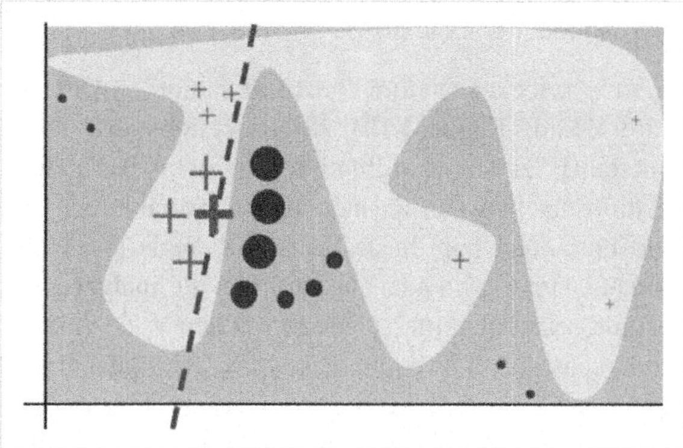

Figure 4.8 Example of Interpretation with a Local Linear Model[6]

Figure 4.7 illustrates an example local explanation of non-linear relationships of two classes: pink and blue areas. The bold red cross is an independent prediction of the pink class that has to be explained. LIME algorithm samples the training observations (z), makes predictions using the $f(z)$ function (e.g. random forest), and creates a local neighborhood, assigning higher weights $\pi_x(z)$ to the nearest predictions (the crosses and dots with bigger size). The dashed line represents local linear model $g(z')$. The creation of local neighborhoods allows one to develop more precise linear explainers. To measure infidelity of the g in approximating f in the locality defined by distance π_x, the LIME algorithm uses locality-aware loss metric (Equation 4.4).

$$\mathcal{L}(f, g, \pi_x) = \sum_{z,z' \in \mathcal{Z}} \pi_x(z)\left(f(z) - g(z')\right)^2 \quad (4.4)$$

[6] Ribeiro et al. (2016) pp. 1138

The goal of the LIME algorithm is to increase interpretability and decrease the complexity of the local explainer, minimizing locality-aware loss and simplifying the model (e.g. decreasing the number of non-zero coefficients of a linear model). The optimization function of the algorithm can be represented in the following way (Equation 4.5).

$$\xi(x) = \underset{g}{\operatorname{argmin}}\ \mathcal{L}(f, g, \pi_x) + \Omega(g) \tag{4.5}$$

where:
$\Omega(g)$ = measure of model complexity

For twelve randomly selected random forest predictions, LIME explainers were developed (Figure 4.9 and Figure 4.10). All predictions have the labels: 0 (non-default) or 1 (default). The blue right-side horizontal bar indicates that there is a positive relationship between an independent variable and a selected class. The red left-side horizontal bar illustrates that there is a negative relationship between a parameter and a dependent group. For all analyzed local explainers, V365 is the most important classifier. Generally, when V365 is lower than 0.1645, it influences the increase of PD; the increase of V365 higher than 0.1645 causes the decrease of PD (in Figure 4.9: cases 3, 5, 6 and in Figure 4.10: cases 2, 3, 5). V757 is another important classifier. V757 has a positive relationship with PD. The borrowers who have V757 values that are higher than −0.146 tend to have higher PD. Values of V757 that are lower than −0.146 reduce PD (in Figure 4.9: cases 1, 2, 3, 5, 6 and in Figure 4.10: cases 1, 3, 5).

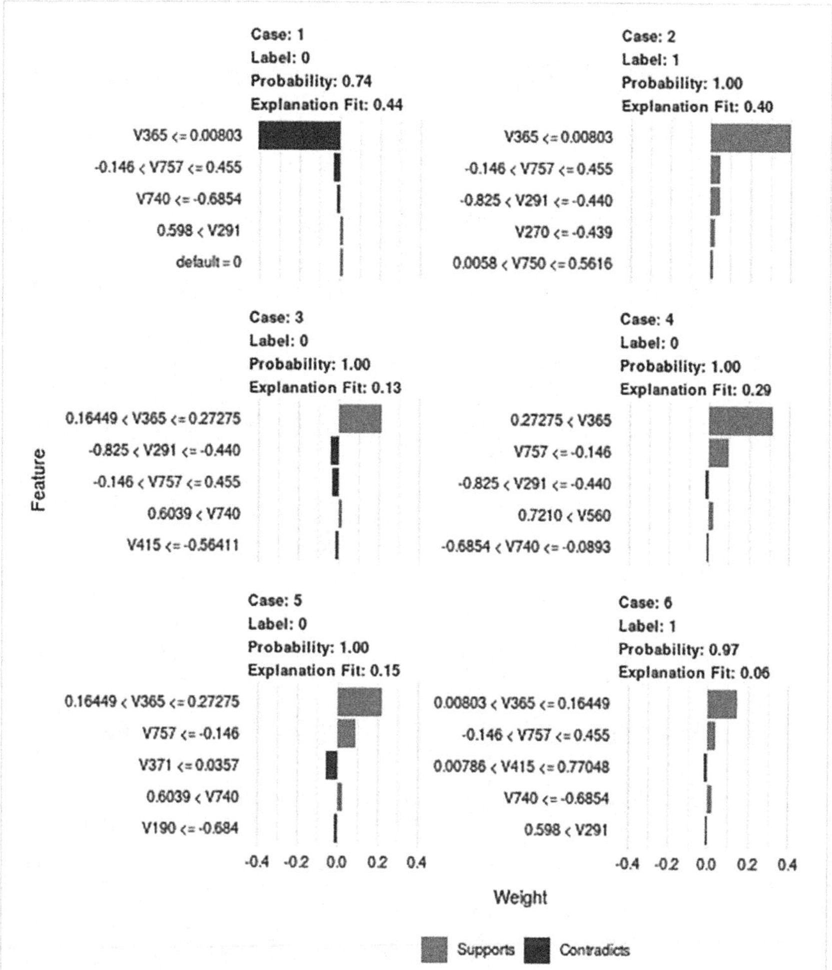

Figure 4.9 LIME Explainers for the Random Forest Model (Sample 1)

Although the LIME method allows one to analyze the variables' impacts for black-box models, it has some limitations. The main assumption of the LIME approach is that an explained model is linear on the local scale. However, for complex non-linear models, this assumption is not always met. Another limitation of the LIME approach is that it can be difficult to understand the global impact

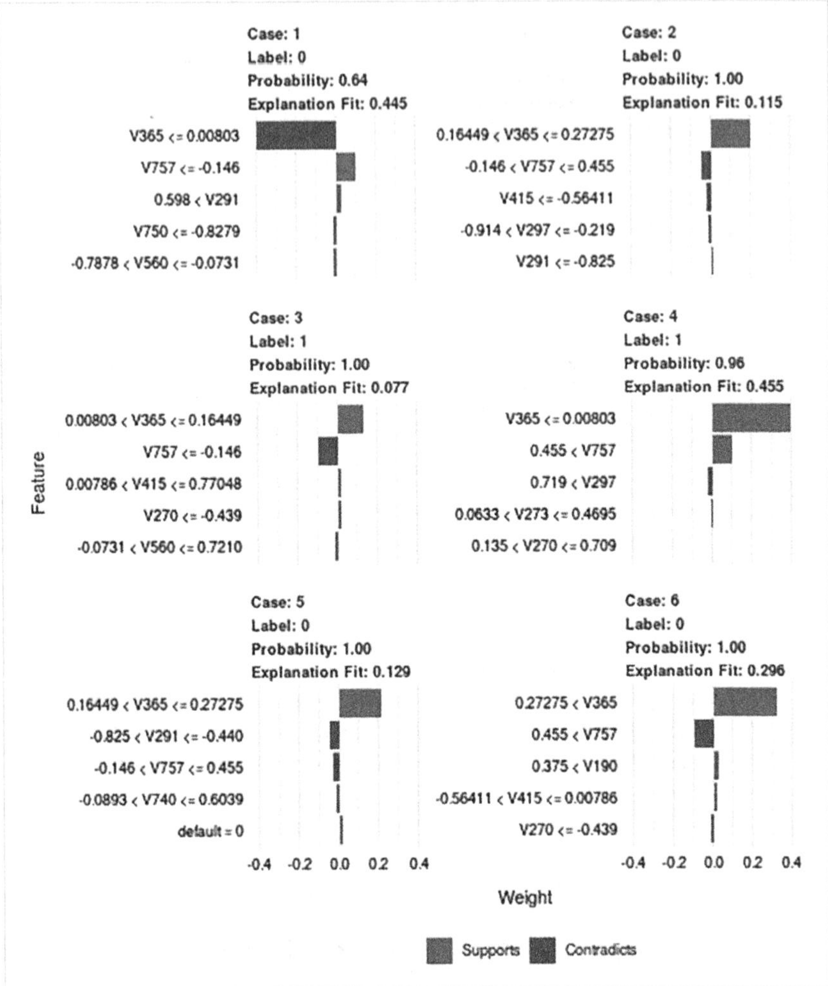

Figure 4.10 LIME Explainers for the Random Forest Model (Sample 2)

of variables from local explanations. Local explanations can significantly vary between each other. In order to make an unbiased analysis of variables' impacts, an analyst has to review and summarize a big number of individual explainers.

4.4.3 Model Performance

All observations that are not included in the bootstrap datasets are used for estimation of out-of-bag error. The out-of-bag score shows the share of misclassified observations in the total number of out-of-bag observations. Out-of-bag error is a metric of in-sample validation because it employs just the training dataset. Figure 4.11 demonstrates the relationships between out-of-bag error and the number of random forest trees. The red line represents the share of misclassified non-default borrowers in the out-of-bag sample. The green line illustrates the out-of-bag error for defaults customers. The black line shows the total out-of-bag error of the model. Within the first hundred decision trees, the out-of-bag error decreases sharply with an increasing number of trees. After 200 decision trees, the addition of new trees does not influence the decrease of out-of-bag error. Consequently, in order to decrease the number of required computation resources for the model, the number of trees has to be reduced from 500 to 200. The final out-of-bag error for non-defaults (nearly 9%) is higher than the error for default observations (around 2%). The total out-of-bag error of the model is at the level of 7%.

Another way to analyze the performance of the random forest model is to develop confusion matrices for in- and out-of-sample classifications (Table 4.13, Table 4.14). All model's estimated PDs (proportions of trees' votes), were converted to the categorical variables. For instance, borrowers with PDs higher than 50% were classified as defaulted; when PDs were equal to or lower than 50%, borrowers were classified as non-defaulted. The confusion matrix for in-sample classification shows that the model misclassified defaults (5.29%) more often than non-default (0.90%). On another hand, out-of-sample validation had a higher error classifying non-defaults (5.21%) than defaults (0.74%). Therefore, it is difficult to determine whether the model is less sensitive to defaults or non-defaults.

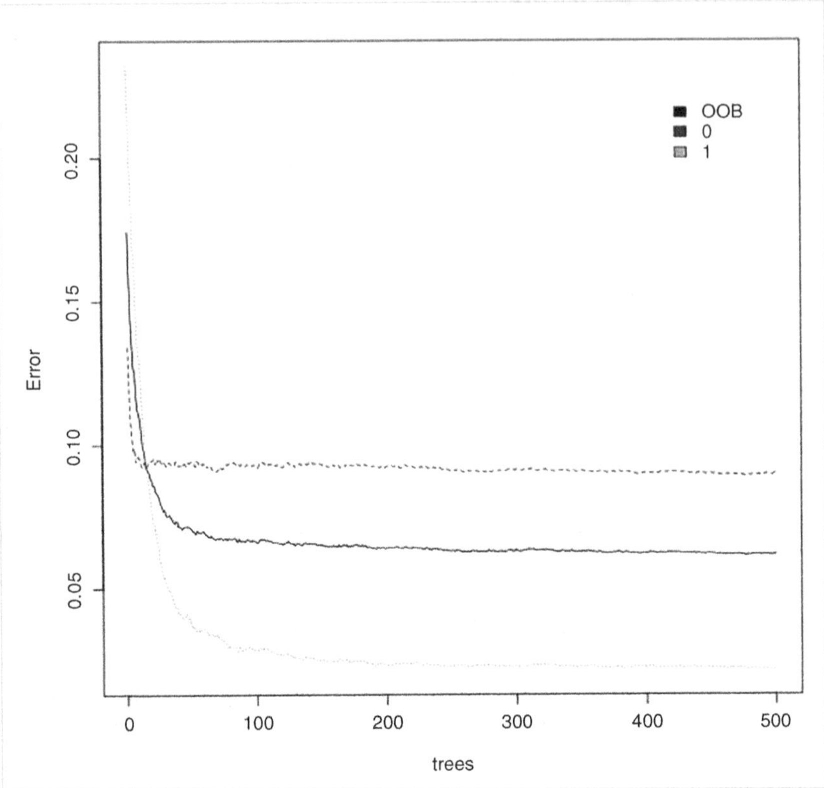

Figure 4.11 Out-Of-Bag Error in Relation to Number of Trees of the Random Forest Model

Table 4.13 Confusion Matrix for In-Sample Classification of the Random Forest Model

	Actual non-default	Actual default
Predicted non-default	8602	850
Predicted default	144	6466

The random forest model has high classification power. For example, the model correctly classified around 94% of borrowers. Out-of-sample validation showed slightly higher classification accuracy and F1-score than in-sample validation. The model sensitivity for the testing data (0.9818) was almost 10% higher

Table 4.14 Confusion Matrix for Out-Of-Sample Classification of the Random Forest Model

	Actual non-default	Actual default
Predicted non-default	3720	51
Predicted default	359	2755

than the sensitivity for the training data (0.8838). At the same time, the model precision for the testing dataset (0.8847) was lower than the precision for the in-sample classification (0.9782). The AUC score of the model was on the level of 97.84%, which illustrates that the model fits the actual data well (Figure 4.12), (Table 4.15).

Table 4.15 Performance Metrics of the Random Forest Model

In-Sample Validation	Out-Of-Sample Validation
Accuracy: 0.9381 Sensitivity: 0.8838 Precision: 0.9782 F1-score: 0.9286	Accuracy: 0.9405 Sensitivity: 0.9818 Precision: 0.8847 F1-score: 0.9307

4.5 Models Comparison

The goal of this section is to compare the performance and interpretability of the models. The models' performance will be evaluated according to the following criteria:

1. the general ability of a model to classify correctly defaults and non-defaults,
2. the ability of a model to identify accurately default borrowers,
3. the robustness of a model when classifying new data.

For the first criteria, the accuracy and AUC metrics of the models can be compared (Table 4.16). Based on the accuracy metric, the random forest model showed the highest performance (nearly 94%). Whereas, logistic regression had an accuracy lower by 6% (approximately 88%). The decision tree classified the observations better than the logit model, but worse than the random forest model. The accuracy of the decision tree model was at the level of 91%.

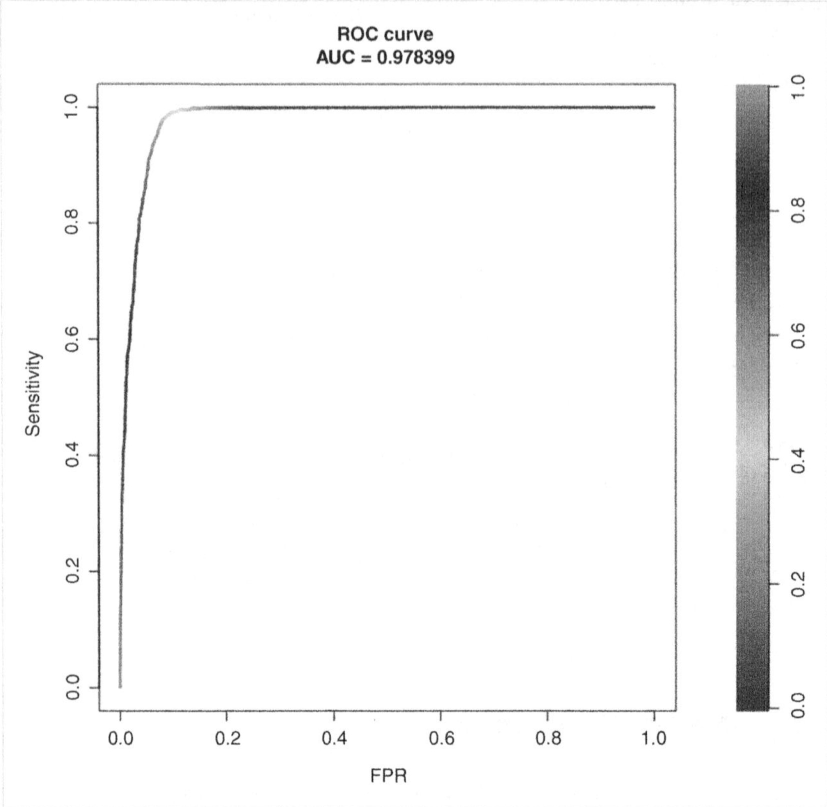

Figure 4.12 ROC Curve for Out-Of-Sample Classification of the Random Forest Model

Table 4.16 Comparison of Goodness of fit of the Models

Validation Data	Metric	Logistic Regression	Decision Tree	Random Forest
In-Sample Validation	Accuracy	0.8783	0.9062	0.9381
	AUC	0.9405	0.9430	0.9778
Out-Of-Sample Validation	Accuracy	0.8840	0.9068	0.9405
	AUC	0.9416	0.9396	0.9782

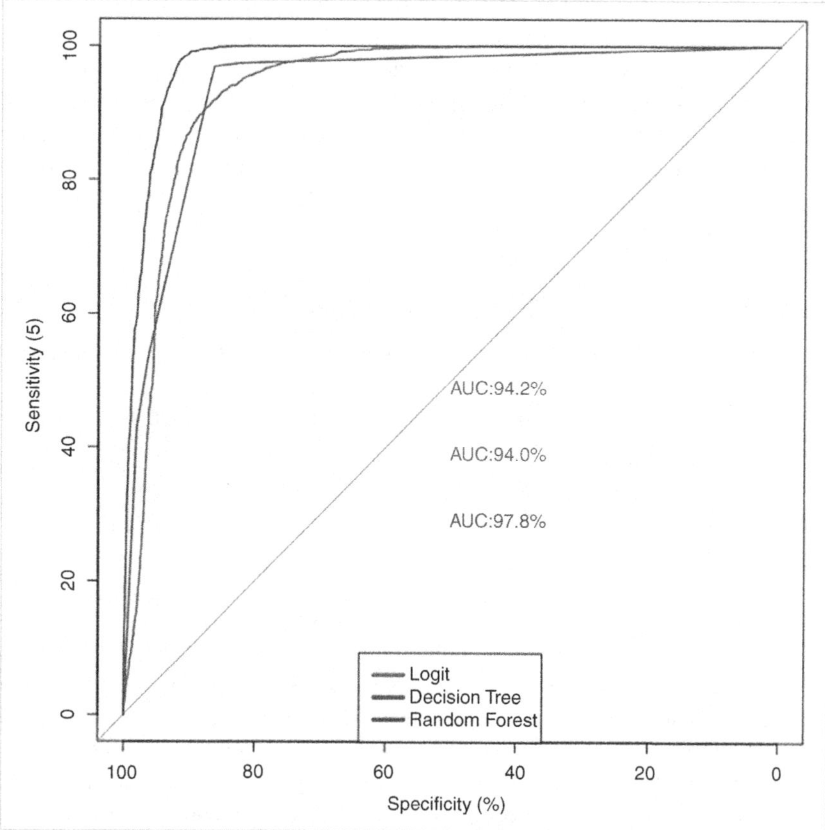

Figure 4.13 ROC Curves for Out-Of-Sample Classifications of the Models

Figure 4.13 illustrates the comparison of ROC curves and AUC values for the models validated on the testing data. Based on the ROC curve analysis, the logistic regression and the decision tree models have similar relationships of sensitivity and specificity (opposite to false positive rate) regarding the cut-off values. Both models have AUC values of around 94%. The random forest model has the highest AUC score (97.8%). Thus, the random forest model is much better than other models, distinguishing between default and non-default classes.

When the model's prediction is non-default, but the actual value is the default, the prediction is considered to be false negative. To reduce credit losses caused by false-negative predictions, the credit scoring model must be accurate in identifying default events. To evaluate the ability of models to classify correctly default borrowers, sensitivity, precision, and F1-score of the models were compared (Table 4.17). The logistic regression model has higher precision (87%) than the decision tree model (83%). However, the overall analysis demonstrates that the machine learning models have higher sensitivity and F1-score values than the logit model. For instance, the random forest has the highest F1-score (approximately 93%).

Table 4.17 Comparison of Correctness of Default Identification of the Models

Validation Data	Metric	Logistic Regression	Decision Tree	Random Forest
In-Sample Validation	Sensitivity	0.8257	0.9731	0.8838
	Precision	0.8717	0.8289	0.9782
	F1-score	0.8481	0.8952	0.9286
Out-Of-Sample Validation	Sensitivity	0.8357	0.9690	0.9818
	Precision	0.8740	0.8305	0.8847
	F1-score	0.8544	0.8944	0.9307

To evaluate the robustness of a model when classifying new data, in-sample and out-of-sample validation results have to be compared. Based on the accuracy ratio, all models performed slightly better within the out-of-sample classification. Based on the F1-score, the logistic regression and random forest models had a higher performance using out-of-sample data. On the other hand, the decision tree model has a slightly worse F1-score in the out-of-sample classification (89.4%) compared to the results in the sample (89.5%). Another factor that makes the decision tree model less robust is that it is based on only three features. If some of these parameters are missing from the new dataset, the decision tree classification will be inconsistent. To summarize, the logit and random forest models were robust in classifying the test data. The decision tree model is less robust compared to other models.

Interpretability is another key characteristic of model quality. Decision tree and logistic regression models are considered interpretable methods. Because the data are standardized, the weights of the logit model parameters can illustrate the magnitude of their impact. The decision tree allows one to trace all steps of classification. Each node of the decision tree is assigned to an independent variable with a certain cut-off value. All default and non-default borrowers are divided by the parameters into groups with a smaller impurity, where one class is more dominant.

Random forest is a black-box model with low interpretability. The random forest model uses the aggregated results of 500 different trees with randomly selected parameters and observations. Therefore, it is more difficult to determine the impact of the independent variables. In order to explain the results of the random forest model, global and local explanation techniques were applied. For the global explanation, the average decrease of Gini impurity for every parameter was estimated. The LIME algorithm was selected as a local explainer. The combination of these two techniques allows one to identify the importance and impact of the model's parameters. However, in a random forest, the interpretation of the model is less explicit than in the logit and decision tree models.

Despite the fact that all models applied different techniques to interpret the results, they identified the same parameters as the most important. For instance, V356 and V757 had the strongest impact in each model. V365 is a dominant risk factor with the highest explanatory power. There is a negative relationship between V365 and the probability of default. Another risk driver is V757. V757 has positive relationships with PD: An increase of V757 causes an increase in the probability of default.

To summarize, the empirical analysis showed that the applied machine learning techniques had better performance than logistic regression in the classification of defaults and non-defaults. The decision tree and random forest models have higher overall classification accuracy and better detection of default events. Nevertheless, the described machine learning methods have some limitations. For instance, the decision tree model is less robust than other approaches, because it uses a significantly lower number of parameters. The complex structure of the random forest significantly reduces the interpretability of this approach. As a result, this method requires the application of additional techniques for interpreting the results.

5 Conclusion

The present research aimed to examine whether AI techniques can effectively predict credit risks of individuals based on the borrowers' financial data. The research question was to determine which method more accurately predicts individual defaults based on the comparison of AI and logit models. In order to answer the research question, theoretical concepts regarding credit scoring were introduced. Furthermore, AI and traditional credit scoring methods were compared by using both theoretical and empirical analysis.

The research presents an analysis of the advantages and disadvantages of traditional credit scoring methods. An expert system is a flexible and well-interpreted analytical tool. The expert system employs both empirical analysis and theoretical experts' knowledge about credit risks. Therefore, the expert systems can be customized to the particular credit product and illustrate linear and nonlinear relationships of data. However, the huge dependence on the knowledge base complicates the development, maintenance, and scaling of an expert system. Linear discriminant analysis and logistic regression are examples of linear models. The parametric representation of these models makes them easy to interpret. When all assumptions of the models are met, these methods can be very efficient in classifying defaults and non-defaults. On another hand, these methods have several disadvantages. For example, both these models cannot describe complex non-linear relationships between independent and dependent variables. Besides, the linear discriminant analysis has several assumptions which can be hardly met (e.g. normal distribution of predictors). Finally, the logistic regression model requires a large size of training data to provide reliable results.

Several AI classification methods were overviewed in this research. The key advantage of most analyzed machine learning methods is that they can describe complex non-linear relationships using different techniques. For instance, decision trees can build complex sequences of connected conditions based on the

B. Popovych, *Application of AI in Credit Scoring Modeling*, BestMasters,
https://doi.org/10.1007/978-3-658-40180-1_5

independent variables. Random forest and gradient boosting are ensemble techniques that aggregate the results of multiple individual decision trees using bagging and boosting algorithms respectively. Deep neural networks are composed of hidden layers of interconnected neurons that process data and transfer the outputs to the next layers. SVM can project the data onto a higher-dimensional space where it is possible to linearly split the data using a hyperplane. K-means clustering splits all data into clusters, maximizing the similarity within the clusters and diversifying the clusters among themselves. The theoretical overview of the machine learning methods has shown that higher performance approaches have lower explainability (e.g. deep neural networks, random forest), while some other methods that are easier to interpret (e.g. decision trees) tend to have lower performance. To verify the above statement and assess the effectiveness of AI in credit scoring, the decision trees, and random forest models were selected for the empirical analysis.

Answering the research question, logistic regression, decision tree, and random forest were compared based on the empirical analysis. Within the analysis, all methods were trained on the financial data of individual borrowers. The training data was composed of transactional, financial, and social-demographic characteristics of the borrowers and their default statuses. The results of the empirical analysis showed that AI methods predicted credit defaults more accurately than the logit model. Based on the accuracy ratio, the random forest outperformed the logistic regression by 6%. The decision tree classified data 2% more accurately than logistic regression. For instance, the accuracy scores of the random forest, decision tree, logit models were equal to 94%, 90%, and 88% respectively. The random forest also had a significantly higher AUC score for the out-of-sample classification (97.8%) than other methods. While the logit and decision tree models had AUC values of around 94%. Moreover, the analysis of models' performances demonstrated that the random forest and decision tree models were more correct in detecting default borrowers. For instance, the F1-scores of the random forest and decision tree models were 93% and 89.5% respectively, whereas the F1-score of the logistic regression was at the level of 85%.

Despite the fact that the random forest and decision trees models had a better performance, the interpretations of these models showed the several limitations of the analyzed methods. The decision tree model is less robust than other approaches. For instance, it uses only 3 predictors for classification that is significantly lower than in the other models. This issue makes the model more sensitive to the structural changes in new data. For example, if some of these 3 parameters are missing from the new data, the decision tree results will be inconsistent.

The results of the random forest model were more difficult to interpret. The output of the random forest is based on the aggregation of 500 decision trees built on randomly selected training data. Thus, to determine the impact of the independent variables, an analyst has to use indirect methods of global and local interpretation. For interpretation of the random forest, LIME explainers were developed and an average decrease of Gini impurity for each predictor was estimated. As a result, the proposed interpretation methods identified the same parameters as the most important, as in the decision tree and logistic regression. However, even using global and local explanations, the random forest model remains less interpretable than the logit and decision tree models.

The advantages of this research lie in its possible application within the credit scoring field. In fact, the AI models analyzed in this thesis could be efficiently applied for the credit risk assessment of individual borrowers. Application of the random forest model can significantly increase the accuracy of credit default predictions compared to the logit model. Better classification of defaults, caused by the random forest application, can decrease the credit losses of a creditor. Furthermore, creditors can enhance the traditional credit scoring analysis, using a decision tree model for illustration of the parameters impacts. However, applying AI methods, creditors have to consider the mentioned robustness and interpretability limitations of the machine learning methods in order to comply with regulatory requirements.

On the other hand, the present research has several limitations. First, only one method of traditional credit scoring was employed in empirical analysis. Logistic regression was selected as a benchmark because, based on the literature overview, several studies in credit scoring prove its high classification power. Furthermore, compared to LDA and linear regression, logit regression has much fewer assumptions to be met. However, this research does not provide empirical evidence that other traditional credit scoring methods, such as discriminant analysis, will be less effective than artificial intelligence methods. Another limitation is regarding the low interpretability of the anonymized dataset. Anonymous column names limited the qualitative analysis of the independent variables. The expert analysis of the parameters could improve the quality of feature selection and the interpretability of the models.

References

Ahelegbey, D. F. / Giudici, P. / Hadji-Misheva, B. (2019): Latent Factor Models for Credit Scoring in P2P Systems, in: Physica A: Statistical Mechanics and its Applications, 522, pp. 112–121, retrieved from https://mpra.ub.uni-muenchen.de/92636/1/MPRA_paper_92636.pdf, assessed January 30, 2021

Akinwande, M. O. / Dikko, H. G. / Samson, A. (2015): Variance Inflation Factor: as a Condition for The Inclusion of Suppressor Variable (s) in Regression Analysis, in: Open Journal of Statistics, 5(07), p. 754, retrieved from https://www.scirp.org/html/11-1240578_62189.htm?pagespeed=noscript, accessed February 16, 2021

Ali, J. / Khan, R. / Ahmad, N. / Maqsood, I. (2012): Random Forests and Decision Trees, in: International Journal of Computer Science Issues (IJCSI), 9(5), p. 272, retrieved from https://citeseerx.ist.psu.edu/viewdoc/download?doi=10.1.1.402.3863&rep=rep1&type=pdf, accessed February 13, 2021

Allen, J. C. (1995): A promise of approvals in minutes, not hours, in: American banker, 28, p. 12, retrieved from https://www.americanbanker.com/news/credit-scoring-a-promise-of-approvals-in-minutes-not-hours, assessed February 1, 2021

Alma, Z. / Mansiya, K. / Torgyn M. / Marzhan, M. / Kanat, N. (2014: The Methodology of Expert Systems, in: International Journal of Computer Science and Network Security (IJCSNS), 14(2), 62–63, retrieved from http://cloud.politala.ac.id/politala/1.%20Jurusan/Teknik%20Informatika/19.%20e-journal/Jurnal%20Internasional%20TI/IJCSNS/2014%20Vol.%2014%20No.%2002/20140209_The%20Methodology%20of%20Expert%20Systems.pdf, accessed February 11, 2021

Altman, E. I. (1968): Financial Ratios, Discriminant Analysis and the Prediction of Corporate Bankruptcy, in: The Journal of Finance, 23(4), pp. 589–609, retrieved from https://www.academia.edu/download/44793197/Altman_1968_Financial_Ratios__Discriminant_Analysis_and_the_Prediction_of_Corporate.pdf, accessed January 28, 2021

Altman, E. I. / Marco, G. / Varetto, F. (1994): Corporate Distress Diagnosis: Comparisons Using Linear Discriminant Analysis and Neural Networks (The Italian Experience), n.p.: Journal of Banking & Finance, 18(3), pp. 505–529.

Baesens, B. / Van Gestel, T. / Viaene, S. / Stepanova, M. / Suykens, J. / Vanthienen, J. (2003): Benchmarking State-of-the-art Classification Algorithms for Credit Scoring, Journal of the Operational Research Society, 54(6), pp. 627–635, retrieved from https://doi.org/10.1057/palgrave.jors.2601545, accessed January 25, 2021

B. Popovych, *Application of AI in Credit Scoring Modeling*, BestMasters, https://doi.org/10.1007/978-3-658-40180-1

Balas, V. E. / Solanki, V. K. / Kumar, R. (2020): An Industrial IoT Approach for Pharmaceutical Industry Growth: Volume 2. Academic Press.

Bank for International Settlements (2021): History of the Basel Committee, retrieved from https://www.bis.org/bcbs/history.htm?m=3%7C14%7C573%7C76, assessed February 1, 2021

Bank of International Settlements (2018): The Rise of Zombie Firms: Causes and Consequences, BIS Quarterly Review, pp. 67–78 retrieved from https://www.bis.org/publ/qtr pdf/r_qt1809g.pdf, accessed January 25, 2021

Bousquet, O. / Boucheron, S. / Lugosi, G. (2003): Introduction to Statistical Learning Theory, In Summer School on Machine Learning (pp. 169–207). Springer, Berlin, Heidelberg, retrieved from http://www.cs.cmu.edu/~10701/slides/Learning_Theory_Notes.pdf, accessed February 9, 2021

Breiman, L. (2001): Random Forests, n.p.: Machine learning, 45(1), pp. 5–32

Bussmann, N. / Giudici / P., Marinelli, D. / Papenbrock, J. (2020): Explainable Machine Learning In Credit Risk Management, n.p.: Computational Economics, pp. 1–14

Campbell, T. S. / Dietrich, J. K. (1983): The Determinants of Default on Insured Conventional Residential Mortgage Loans, in: the Journal of Finance, 38(5), pp. 1569–1581, retrieved from https://www.jstor.org/stable/2327587, accessed January 29, 2021

Charitou, A. / Neophytou, E. / Charalambous, C. (2004): Predicting Corporate Failure: Empirical Evidence for the UK, in: European Accounting Review, 13(3), pp. 465–497, retrieved from https://www.researchgate.net/publication/24080149_Predicting_corp orate_failure_empirical_evidence_for_the_UK, accessed January 29, 2021

Charter of Fundamental Rights of the European Union (2000): Official Journal of the European Union, C 326/391, 2012/C 326/02, retrieved from https://eur-lex.europa.eu/legal-content/EN/TXT/?uri=CELEX:12012P/TXT, accessed January 28, 2021

Chong, I. G. / Jun, C. H. (2005): Performance of Some Variable Selection Methods When Multicollinearity is Present, in: Chemometrics and Intelligent laboratory systems, 78(1–2), 103–112, retrieved from http://automatica.dei.unipd.it/public/Schenato/PSC/2010_2 011/gruppo4-Building_termo_identification/IdentificazioneTermodinamica20072008/ Biblio/Biblio-PLS/Performance%20of%20some%20variable%20selection%20meth ods%20when%20multicollinearity.pdf, accessed February 17, 2021

Deloitte (2020): Artificial Intelligence for Credit Risk Management, France, retrieved from https://www2.deloitte.com/content/dam/Deloitte/fr/Documents/risk/Publications/del oitte_artificial-intelligence-credit-risk.pdf, accessed January 25, 2021

Desai, V. S. / Crook, J. N. / Overstreet Jr, G. A. (1996): A Comparison of Neural Networks and Linear Scoring Models in the Credit Union Environment. European Journal of Operational Research, 95(1), pp. 24–37, retrieved from https://www.researchgate.net/profile/ George_Overstreet/publication/223603370_A_comparison_of_neural_network_and_ linear_scoring_models_in_credit_union_environment/links/5a956bb745851535bcdc8 bd0/A-comparison-of-neural-network-and-linear-scoring-models-in-credit-union-enviro nment.pdf, assessed February 2, 2021

DeVaney, S. A. (1994): The Usefulness of Financial Ratios as Predictors of Household Insolvency: Two Perspectives, in: Financial Counseling and Planning, 5(1), pp. 5–24, retrieved from https://citeseerx.ist.psu.edu/viewdoc/download?doi=10.1.1.456.7138& rep=rep1&type=pdf, assessed January 30, 2021

Durand, D. (1941): Risk Elements in Consumer Installment Financing, National Bureau of Economic Research, New York, retrieved from https://dspace.gipe.ac.in/xmlui/bitstream/handle/10973/25006/GIPE-061767.pdf?sequence=3&isAllowed=y, accessed January 26, 2021

Efron, B. / Tibshirani, R. (1997): Improvements on Cross-Validation: The 632+ Bootstrap Method, in: Journal of the American Statistical Association, 92(438), pp. 548–560, retrieved from http://cindy.informatik.uni-bremen.de/cosy/teaching/CM_2011/Eval3/efron_97.pdf, accessed February 15, 2021

Equal Credit Opportunity Act (1976): United States Law, codified as 15 U.S.C. § 1691, retrieved from https://uscode.house.gov/view.xhtml?req=granuleid%3AUSC-prelim-title15-chapter41-subchapter4&edition=prelim, accessed January 28, 2021

Fair Credit Reporting Act (1970): United States Law, codified as 15 U.S.C. § 1681, retrieved from https://www.ftc.gov/system/files/documents/statutes/fair-credit-reporting-act/545a_fair-credit-reporting-act-0918.pdf, accessed January 29, 2021

Fair Isaac Corporation (2018): The History of the FICO Score, retrieved from https://www.myfico.com/credit-education/blog/history-of-the-fico-score, assessed January 29, 2021

Fair Isaac Corporation (2020): What's in my FICO Scores, retrieved from https://www.myfico.com/credit-education/whats-in-your-credit-score, assessed January 30, 2021

Fathi, E. / Shoja, B. M. (2018): Deep Neural Networks for Natural Language Processing. In Handbook of statistics (Vol. 38, pp. 229–316). Elsevier

Fisher, Ronald A. (1936): The Use of Multiple Measurements in Taxonomic Problems, in: Annals of Eugenics, 7 (2), pp. 179–188, retrieved from https://onlinelibrary.wiley.com/doi/epdf/10.1111/j.1469-1809.1936.tb02137.x, accessed January 26, 2021

Friedman, J. / Hastie, T. / Tibshirani, R. (2001): The Elements of Statistical Learning (Vol. 1, No. 10), New York, in Springer Series in Statistics, retrieved from https://books.google.at/books?hl=en&lr=&id=tVIjmNS3Ob8C&oi=fnd&pg=PR13&dq=hastie+tibshirani+friedman&ots=EOCeJ7I506&sig=H57rwpe2_QJEqAcI_0sJOIySGCg&redir_esc=y#v=onepage&q=tree&f=false, accessed February 7, 2021

Frydman, H. / Altman, E. I. / Kao, D. L. (1985): Introducing Recursive Partitioning for Financial Classification: The Case of Financial Distress, in: The Journal of Finance, 40(1), pp. 269–291, retrieved from https://www.jstor.org/stable/2328060, assessed January 30, 2021

Gardner, M. J. / Mills, D. L. (1989): Evaluating the Likelihood of Default on Delinquent Loans, in: Financial Management, pp. 55–63, retrieved from https://www.jstor.org/stable/3665797, accessed January 29, 2021

General Data Protection Regulation (2016): General Data Protection Regulation - GDPR, updated on 04.05.2016, retrieved from https://gdpr-info.eu/art-4-gdpr/, assessed February 4, 2021

Gunning, D. / Aha, D. (2019): DARPA's Explainable Artificial Intelligence (XAI) Program, in: AI Magazine, 40(2), pp. 44–58, retrieved from https://ojs.aaai.org/index.php/aimagazine/article/view/2850/3419, accessed February 8, 2021

He, H. / Garcia, E. A. (2009): Learning from Imbalanced Data in IEEE Transactions on Knowledge and Data Engineering, 21(9), pp. 1263–1284, n.p.

Henley, W. E., Hand, D. J. (1996): AK-Nearest-Neighbour Classifier for Assessing Consumer Credit Risk, in Journal of the Royal Statistical Society: Series D (The Statistician), 45(1), pp. 77–95, retrieved from https://pages.ucsd.edu/~aronatas/project/academic/Nearest%20neighbor%20analysis%20in%20credit%20scoring.pdf, assessed January 30, 2021

Ibrahim, M. (2019): Reducing Correlation of Random Forest-Based Learning-to-Rank Algorithms Using Subsample Size, in: Computational Intelligence, 35(4), pp. 774–798, n.p.

IFRS 9 (2018): IFRS 9 Financial Instruments, retrieved from https://www.ifrs.org/issued-standards/list-of-standards/ifrs-9-financial-instruments/#about, assessed February 3, 2021

Investopedia (2020): Credit Score, retrieved from https://www.investopedia.com/terms/c/credit_score.asp, assessed January 29, 2021

Liong, C. Y. / Foo, S. F. (2013, April): Comparison of Linear Discriminant Analysis and Logistic Regression for Data Classification, in: AIP Conference Proceedings (Vol. 1522, No. 1, pp. 1159–1165), American Institute of Physics, retrieved from https://www.researchgate.net/file.PostFileLoader.html?id=54e22d84d4c1184c7f8b45b4&assetKey=AS:273713902096384@1442269888002, accessed February 10, 2021

McFadden, D. (1974): Conditional Logit Analysis of Qualitative Choice Behavior, Frontiers in Economics, P. Zarembka, eds. New York: Academic Press

Perez, L. V. (2017): Principal Component Analysis to Address Multicollinearity, Walla Walla: Whitman College, retrieved from https://www.whitman.edu/Documents/Academics/Mathematics/2017/Perez.pdf, accessed February 17, 2021

Raileanu, L. E. / Stoffel, K. (2004): Theoretical Comparison between the Gini Index and Information Gain Criteria in Annals of Mathematics and Artificial Intelligence, 41(1), pp. 77–93

Ribeiro, M. T. / Singh, S. / Guestrin, C. (2016): "Why Should I Trust You?"—Explaining the Predictions of any Classifier, in Proceedings of the 22nd ACM SIGKDD International Conference on Knowledge Discovery and Data Mining, pp. 1135–1144, retrieved from https://arxiv.org/pdf/1602.04938.pdf?ref=morioh.com, accessed February 25, 2021

S&P Global Ratings (2020): European Corporate Credit Outlook 2020: In the Balance, retrieved from https://www.spglobal.com/_assets/documents/ratings/research/european-corporate-credit-outlook-2020-in-the-balance.pdf, accessed January 25, 2021

Schreiber-Gregory, D. (2018): Logistic and Linear Regression Assumptions: Violation Recognition and Control, Henry M Jackson Foundation, retrieved from https://www.researchgate.net/publication/341354759_Logistic_and_Linear_Regression_Assumptions_Violation_Recognition_and_Control, accessed February 11, 2021

Sharma, A. (2020): Decision Tree vs. Random Forest—Which Algorithm Should you Use?, Analytics Vidhya, Gurgaon, retrieved from https://www.analyticsvidhya.com/blog/2020/05/decision-tree-vs-random-forest-algorithm/, accessed February 10, 2021

Steyerberg, E. W. / Harrell Jr, F. E. / Borsboom, G. J. / Eijkemans, M. J. C. / Vergouwe, Y. / Habbema, J. D. F. (2001): Internal Validation of Predictive Models: Efficiency of Some Procedures for Logistic Regression Analysis, in: Journal of Clinical Epidemiology, 54(8), pp. 774–781, retrieved from https://www.southalabama.edu/mathstat/personal_pages/mulekar/BUS622/Steyerberg-2001.pdf, accessed February 16, 2021

Suykens, J. A. (2001, May): Nonlinear Modelling and Support Vector Machines, in IMTC proceedings of the 18th IEEE Instrumentation and Measurement Technology Conference, Rediscovering Measurement in the age of Informatics (Cat. No. 01CH 37188) (Vol. 1, pp. 287–294). IEEE, retrieved from https://www.researchgate.net/profile/Johan_Suykens/publication/3899462_Nonlinear_modelling_and_support_vector_machines/links/00b495241434e95946000000.pdf, accessed February 13, 2021

The Basel Framework (2021): The Standards of the Basel Committee on Banking Supervision updated on 22 January 2021, retrieved from https://www.bis.org/basel_framework/index.htm?m=3%7C14%7C697, assessed February 2, 2021

Tripathi, K. P. (2011): A Review on Knowledge-Based Expert System: Concept and Architecture, in: IJCA Special Issue on Artificial Intelligence Techniques-Novel Approaches & Practical Applications, 4, pp. 19–23, retrieved from http://citeseerx.ist.psu.edu/viewdoc/download?doi=10.1.1.206.3352&rep=rep1&type=pdf, accessed February 12, 2021

Wang, J. / Wu, X. / Zhang, C. (2005): Support Vector Machines Based on K-Means Clustering for Real-Time Business Intelligence Systems, in International Journal of Business Intelligence and Data Mining, 1(1), pp. 54–64, retrieved from http://citeseerx.ist.psu.edu/viewdoc/download?doi=10.1.1.96.7836&rep=rep1&type=pdf, accessed January 25, 2021

X. Du / Y. Cai / S. Wang / L. Zhang (2016): Overview of Deep Learning, 31st Youth Academic Annual Conference of Chinese Association of Automation (YAC), Wuhan, China, 2016, pp. 159–164, retrieved from http://pages.erau.edu/~andrewsa/sci_fi_projects_spring_2019/Project_2/Chin_Matthew/Chin_Project2_HU338/Du_Cai.pdf, accessed February 13, 2021

Ye, J. / Chow, J.-H. / Chen, J. / Zheng, Z. (2009): Stochastic Gradient Boosted Distributed Decision Trees, in: Proceedings of the 18th ACM conference on Information and knowledge management, (Hong Kong: ACM), pp. 2061–2064, retrieved from https://citeseerx.ist.psu.edu/viewdoc/download?doi=10.1.1.726.9475&rep=rep1&type=pdf, accessed February 12, 2021

Zhao, J. (2017): Machine Learning: Challenges, Lessons, and Opportunities in Credit Risk Modeling, Moody's Analytics Risk Perspectives—Managing Disruption, retrieved from https://www.moodysanalytics.com/risk-perspectives-magazine/managing-disruption/spotlight/machine-learning-challenges-lessons-and-opportunities-in-credit-risk-modeling, accessed January 25, 2021

Made in the USA
Monee, IL
19 October 2026

66037585R00056